PREPARING
EMPLOYEES
FOR
CHANGE

THE PATH OF LEAST RESISTANCE

KEN HULTMAN

LEARNING
CONCEPTS

Library of Congress Cataloging in Publication Data

Hultman, Kenneth E
 The Path of Least Resistance

 1. Organizational change. 2. Organizational behavior. I. Title.
HD58.8.H84   658.4'06   79-11178
 ISBN 0-89384-046-7

Learning Concepts
2501 N. Lamar
Austin, Texas 78705

First Printing, June 1979

Edited by Larry N. Davis

Cover design by Suzanne Pustejovsky
Inside design by Mary Ann Noretto

To my mother and father
who helped me develop a set of beliefs
as a child that I can use as an adult
and
To Pat and Jennifer
for allowing me to pursue the
greatest values that life has to offer.

CONTENTS

So You Want to Make Some Changes?

There are many who would contend that change is about the only thing you can be sure of in life. That's perhaps too optimistic. I have come to believe that there is nothing quite as sure as resistance. Anyone who has ever tried to "make some changes" needs no introduction to resistance. Managers and supervisors are people who often find the need to change things — to try to make them work better — and who just as often find themselves face to face with opposition. Any person, living and active, will find relevance in this book, but it was written with frustrated, and sometimes exasperated, managers and supervisors in mind.

For instance, as a supervisor, you may want to make a relatively simple change, such as moving an employee to another desk, increasing the extent to which employees suggest new ideas, getting them to make better use of time, improving cooperation among employees, transfering them from one department to another, or helping them recognize and fully develop their skills. On the other hand, as a manager, you may want to do something more complex, such as modifying the criteria for promotion, implementing an affirmative action plan, placing one department under another, or abandoning one system of management in favor of another. Although the type of change may vary tremendously, it always seems like resistance is just around the corner, waiting for an opportunity to pounce on best-laid plans.

I once spent hours being annoyed that I had to constantly contend with resistance. Then it finally occurred to me that my resentment wasn't getting me anywhere; in fact, it was greatly interfering with my ability to do anything constructive about resistance. I concluded that a more rational approach was in order and began to piece together ideas for dealing with it. After a few victories, battling resistance actually became somewhat enjoyable. I can't say that I like resistance, but if it didn't exist this book would be unnecessary. Also, when I look back on my career, it seems somewhat ironic that resistance, the enemy of many, has provided direction and purpose to much of my professional activity. I am, nevertheless, dedicated to the eradication of this barrier to constructive change.

This book was written particularly for supervisors and managers, in any job setting, who believe that they have a responsibility to initiate change that has a positive impact on all those affected by it. Anyone who regards fostering constructive change as impossible for them, and uses this belief to justify sitting back and doing nothing, will have little to gain from reading further. Fortunately, I have found that most supervisors and managers are genuinely concerned about the impact of their decisions on others. The problem is seldom with managers' intentions — it is with their lack of knowledge and skills in this area. Many excellent books describe the change process, and although most of these books indicate that resistance must be dealt with, they don't say enough about how this can be done. My goal is to help fill this gap by outlining in detail one approach for overcoming resistance.

The title of this book was chosen after considerable deliberation. We usually think of the "path of least resistance" as action selected by someone not because it's the best, but simply because it's the easiest. As a result, something negative is implied when this phrase is used. If you want to change something, preparing the way so that resistance can be minimized is not only the easiest course but also the best. In your efforts to do something different, it is worth your time to search for the path of least resistance.

It is extremely rare for a manager to do something deliberately to cause resistance. Instead, resistance is almost always the unintended consequence of a manager's actions. After resistance surfaces, most managers aren't sure where it came from or what to do about it. Inevitably, this leads to considerable frustration and many unnecessary failures. This book outlines a model designed to help you establish and maintain more effective working relationships with employees under normal conditions, so that less resistance will exist during periods of change. It also provides a method for identifying and dealing with resistance if it is encountered.

While the model presented here is fairly complex, understanding it requires no specialized knowledge or vocabulary. It will require some work on your part, but once this is mastered you will possess knowledge and skills ready to assist you in handling a wide range of problems. Of course, no model is a panacea which will be equally effective under all circumstances and this one is no exception. You can expect the approach which I describe to be most useful in dealing with resistance as it occurs in individual employees and small work groups. As the number of people involved increases and the complexity of the change expands, the model will become more difficult to apply. Therefore, the methods will probably have limited application to situations involving large-scale changes, such as modifying the structure of a large organization, merging one company with another, or discontinuing a line of products. This qualification notwithstanding, there is no hard and fast rule for determining when a situation is beyond the scope of the model. I encourage you to use your imagination in applying the techniques I present.

Although a problem may be straightforward and simple, sometimes resistance will persist in spite of all your efforts. I can't give you a guarantee that my model will work, even in situations which clearly lend themselves to its use. Our knowledge of human behavior is too imprecise for me or anyone else to offer such a guarantee. What I can do, however, is provide you with some tools which I have found effective in increasing one's chances of successfully dealing with resistance. We may not be able to completely eliminate resistance, but we should be able to improve our odds in combating it.

To facilitate your development of knowledge and skills, the book is broken down into four parts. The first two parts are oriented toward providing you with an understanding of the origins of resistance. Part I deals with the primary components of personality I have found helpful in discovering the meaning of human behavior. Part II presents a discussion of conceptual material related to the change process and resistance.

The last two parts apply the principles outlined in the first two. Part III is intended to increase your skills in identifying the specific causes of resistance. Part IV outlines the resistance strategy model, which is designed to help you develop and implement strategies for dealing with resistance, and then gives several case examples of how the methods in the book have been successfully applied. The overall objective is to increase the probability that you can formulate and use effective strategies for preventing or eliminating resistance to constructive change.

Some people may view this material as an effort to help supervisors and managers become more manipulative in their dealings with employees and, therefore, be critical of the approach. I don't see anything wrong with manipulation, per se. Any time we choose one form of behavior over another in order to have an impact on the behavior of others, we are being manipulative. In my view, behavior should be evaluated by its results. This is certainly not an invitation to inflict pain and fear in the name of some so-called worthy cause. I regard manipulation as being negative when it has inhibiting or destructive consequences for other people. Since it is virtually impossible to make a decision as a manager without manipulating your employees, the techniques I present are designed to help you make your impact as constructive as possible.

I would like to acknowledge those who have been instrumental in helping me with this book. I was fortunate enough to meet Stu Meyers in 1969. We combined his interest in group process with my interest in human values in writing a joint doctoral dissertation. I am indebted to him for extending my thinking about the impact that people have on one another. The excellent graduate education I received at Rutgers University under the guidance of Rob Whiteley and Bill Bingham provided me with both the conceptual tools and incentive to help people solve problems. While I was on the faculty of Florida State University, Steve Wilkerson and I intended to write a book similar to this one, directed toward another audience. Although we went separate ways, our many early-morning brainstorming sessions helped me crystallize my thinking.

When I moved to Austin, I met Larry Davis, who not only told me I should write the book, but introduced me to Ray Bard, president of Learning Concepts. Larry persuaded me to put my volumes of rough notes into some readable form, and was of great assistance as editor for the book. My wife, Pat, who is a very gifted writer, not only spent many hours reviewing the first draft of the manuscript, but also was a constant source of encouragement, support, and love throughout the project. And, finally, I would like to express my appreciation to Sylvia Wyatt, who did an excellent job of typing and retyping the manuscript.

KENNETH E. HULTMAN

PART I

Making Sense out of Human Behavior

Introduction 1

Consider these predicaments:

At a staff meeting everyone verbally agrees to utilize a new procedure, but several weeks later you discover that the procedure has not been implemented.

An employee tells you that career advancement is very important but avoids opportunities for promotion.

Two employees have a problem cooperating, but every time you try to help them the problem gets worse.

A group of employees compliment you on a change in policy but criticize the change behind your back.

Your staff agrees on the main issues involved in a proposed change, but get so bogged down in minor disagreements that the idea is eventually dropped.

Great tension among your employees is interfering with production, but after considerable work you are unable to locate the cause of tension.

Have you ever faced situations like these and wondered what to do? If so, you are not alone. Every supervisor or manager is confronted with situations difficult to understand and even more difficult to deal with. The purpose of this book is to help you increase your knowledge of change and resistance and skills in handling predicaments of this kind.

People don't usually spend a great deal of time thinking about why they do what they do. Nor do they concern themselves very much with the reasons for the behavior of others. Most of us are able to go through life without finding it necessary to understand the origins of human behavior. As a manager or supervisor, however, it is imperative that you understand the behavior of your employees. You have definite responsibilities which require you to get work done through other people. The better you understand them, the more effective you will be in dealing with resistance.

Perhaps the most basic statement we can make about human behavior is that it is purposeful. The purpose of all behavior is to meet needs. Human needs can be divided into two major categories, survival needs and growth needs. Survival needs, which must be met to insure that the species will continue to exist and reproduce itself, include food, water, shelter, safety, sleep, sex, and so on. Growth needs have to do with psychological development and include emotional security, love, belonging, approval from others, recognition, self-worth, creativity, and so on. Survival needs usually take precedence over growth needs. A person starving to death has little time to worry about approval from others or creativity. Meeting survival needs is necessary for there to be any life at all, but the way growth needs are met determines the quality of life. Everything we do is designed to meet one or more of our needs. Without needs there would be no behavior, because needs supply the necessary motivation to act. The wide variety of behavior that people engage in demonstrates the many alternative ways available to meet needs. The quest to meet needs is relentless. No sooner is one need met than another clamors for fulfillment. If you ever get frustrated because of all the time and effort that meeting needs takes, it may be helpful to remember that to be without needs is to be dead.

The way that people go about dealing with their needs is a key factor in the development of personality. Right after birth, an infant begins this lifelong journey of meeting needs. The needs of an infant are relatively simple and occur on a more or less routine basis. A full stomach, a dry diaper, sufficient sleep, and nurturing parents encompass most of the child's requirements for living. The other significant factor about infancy is that the young child is completely dependent on other people for the satisfaction of his or her needs. As the child begins to grow, however, not only do needs become more complex, but the ability to meet needs through independent action becomes greater. Ideally, this process results in a healthy, well-adjusted adult who is capable of mobilizing the necessary resources to respond to the demands of everyday life.

People vary tremendously, however, in their ability to carry out the various functions of adulthood. Some can respond effectively under the most demanding circumstances, while others have difficulty coping with even small changes. The reason for this is that a very complex relationship exists between a person's needs and the behavior intended to meet those needs. Needs, of course, are stimuli, and behavior is the response to those stimuli, but there is no automatic relationship between needs (stimuli) and the behavior designed to meet them. During this chain of events a very improtant phenomenon takes place — thinking. It is the thinking process which largely determines how need-fulfilling behavior is planned, organized, and executed.

The capacity to think is made possible by the human brain, which must be classified as one of the marvels of the universe. Of course, people frequently accuse one another, and at times justifiably so, of not using their brains. We all know what is meant by the expressions, "You don't have a brain in your head" and "What a lame-brain you are." These and similar statements are a rather unflattering way of telling others that the thought process behind their actions leaves something to be desired. Although such expressions are usually spoken during times of anger or frustration, they clearly point out that people expect each other to make intelligent use of their brains before behaving.

In my efforts to show how people use their brains to meet needs, I searched for some useful concepts which would allow me to describe and explain a great deal about how people think and behave, without getting bogged down in too much theory. My objectives were to (1) demonstrate that a strong relationship exists between thinking and doing which could be readily understood and (2) show that knowledge of this relationship is useful in developing one's skills in effectively dealing with resistance to change. After several years of inquiry, I finally hit upon two concepts which provided the foundation I was looking for. These concepts are human *beliefs* and *values*. Beliefs and values have been discussed for thousands of years and receive special attention in current theories and research. In spite of this, not nearly enough has been done to apply what we know about beliefs and values to the problem of dealing with resistance to change. In the pages that follow, I will describe in detail, with specific examples, the ways in which your employees' current beliefs and values may cause them to resist the changes you want to make. I will also attempt to demonstrate that changes in beliefs and values are often required before employees will cooperate with changes proposed by managers and supervisors. We will begin our quest to understand resistance by reviewing each of these concepts in some detail.

You Are What You **2** *Believe*

When people were becoming nutrition conscious, the expression "you are what you eat" was popular, and about physical attributes this is probably true. When we consider the attributes of one's thinking and the thinking process itself, however, *you are what you believe.*

The concept of belief is as old as humanity. You'd think by now we'd have a thorough understanding of beliefs and how they affect behavior. However, we are just beginning to appreciate the profound role that beliefs play in everyday life. We don't even have a clear concensus on a definition of belief. If you asked a hundred people at random for a definition of the term *belief*, you could get one hundred different answers. Some people would define beliefs in terms of religious convictions. Others would say they have to do with purposes or causes to which one is willing to dedicate time or money, while still others would contend that beliefs are opinions. Also, people frequently assume that believing is synonymous with sensing, perceiving, thinking, and feeling. In fact, all these terms are commonly used interchangeably when people say, "I sense that the two of you disagree . . .," "My perception of the situation is . . .," "I think we ought to . . .," "My feeling is that we should consider . . ." When this happens, any distinctive role played by human beliefs becomes obscure.

If this problem was purely one of semantics, there probably wouldn't be much need for serious concern. Yet many people are unaware that a very complex and important relationship exists between their beliefs and how they think, feel, and act. It is not too difficult to understand this, however, since all societies do a relatively poor job of teaching people about these relationships, and ours is certainly no exception. Generally, we devote more attention to providing children with lots of facts, many of questionable usefulness, rather than helping them learn about the process of living. This leads one to question the priorities assigned to various aspects of human development. The relationship between believing and behaving is surely one of the most important factors in understanding human functioning. But as incredible as it may seem, we leave the development of this understanding almost entirely to chance. It is no wonder that so many people experience serious problems in living — they don't fully comprehend the causes of their own behavior. As a manager you probably wouldn't need to concern yourself with these matters if it wasn't for one very relevant factor: these people end up coming to work for you!

Let's begin tackling this issue by first reviewing how the human mind works and then defining the term *belief*. To begin with, people receive information about themselves and the external world through the five senses of seeing, hearing, feeling, smelling, and tasting. Following this, they process the information, organize it, and store it in their brain for future reference. In order to do this, people rely upon their capacity to formulate beliefs.

A belief is a mental construct which allows a person to interpret past and present experiences, and predict what will happen in the future. There are two major types of beliefs: *descriptive beliefs*, which are interpretations regarding what is correct or incorrect, and *evaluative beliefs*, which are interpretations about what is good or bad (Rokeach, 1968). Beliefs define for a person both what *is* and *what is possible.*

Since people have millions of experiences, they develop a great many beliefs. Some examples of beliefs include:

- The door will always open when I turn the knob.
- This chair will always support my weight when I sit down.
- Everyone should always report to work on time.
- I can do this job.
- Working conditions will improve after this contract dispute is resolved.
- Other people are basically honest.
- I believe in equal opportunity for everyone, regardless of race, color, or creed.
- The free enterprise system is good.
- Democracy is the best political system.
- The outlook for the future is very bright.
- Life is worth living.
- I believe there is a God.

Note how these examples of beliefs increase in degree of abstractness. The contents of a person's beliefs, which cover all aspects of one's life, range from the mundane to the very philosophical. These differences are important to keep in mind because beliefs tend to become more resistant to change as they increase in abstractness.

There is a strong connection between the cognitive process of believing, on the one hand, and both feelings and behavior, on the other. Beliefs allow people to attach meaning to life events. As this happens, beliefs stimulate the physiological responses we refer to as feelings or emotions. Beliefs are capable of eliciting any feeling from elation to despair. Typically, there is a close association between the content of beliefs and corresponding feelings. Thus, positive beliefs elicit good feelings, such as exhilaration, joy, and happiness, while negative beliefs elicit bad feelings, such as sorrow, depression, and anger.

It would be difficult to underestimate the relationship which exists between beliefs and behavior. People are motivated to meet their various survival and growth needs. In their attempts to do this, people must learn what to expect from others and from the environment. As they begin to have experiences, people start to formulate interpretations (beliefs) about the meaning of those experiences. Interpretations regarding the past and present are then used to develop other beliefs which help people anticipate or predict what will happen in the future. Without beliefs people would have no way of predicting that one set of actions might lead to positive results, while another set of actions might lead to negative results. The inability to do this would greatly interfere with efforts to successfully engage in need-fulfilling behavior. The impact of beliefs on behavior is one of the major themes of this book, because resistance can often be traced back to the beliefs people hold. Beliefs are subjective interpretations. Often peoples' beliefs are inaccurate.

"Just Because You Believe It, Doesn't Make It Fact"

It is important to make a clear distinction between beliefs and facts. A *fact* is something that can be proven with absolute certainty, while a belief is a subjective interpretation or prediction. People frequently confuse beliefs with facts by making statements like "I know such and so," when they really should say, "I believe . . ." There are many things you can know with certainty and legitimately refer to as facts. For example, you can know your name, age, marital status, and other vital statistics. You can also know that you own a Chevrolet, work at a certain company, and broke your leg five years ago. You can know what you believe and what you regard as important in life. It is accurate to state as a fact "I know I believe people are basically honest," and to state as a belief "I believe people are basically honest," but inaccurate to say "I know people are basically honest," which is a belief stated as a fact. Once you go beyond what you can prove, you're in the realm of belief.

Two areas important in differentiating facts from beliefs have to do with how we view ourselves and other people. You can't know for a fact that you are a worthwhile human being. How you regard yourself as a person stems from beliefs which you have acquired from interpreting experiences. In fact, your self-concept can be defined as all those beliefs, both positive and negative, that you hold regarding yourself. It is not uncommon, however, for people to make such remarks as "I know I'm not very smart" or "I can do anything I set my mind to." Although stated as facts, such statements are actually beliefs about the self.

Similarly, people formulate beliefs about others which are presented as facts. If for example, one of your employees, Diane, said, "David will never make a good supervisor," she would be conveying a belief which in her mind carries the weight of a fact. It is often more accurate to say something like, "Based on what I observed yesterday and last week, it is my belief that he will never be sensitive enough to other people's needs to make a good supervisor." This allows you and others involved to explore the specific reasons for her opinion and to plan actions for dealing with the situation.

When beliefs are presented as facts they are much less amenable to change because they come across as absolute and unchangeable conclusions. Saying that an employee is incapable implies that he or she will always be this way. Unfortunately, many beliefs about others are held as facts, making it difficult to either validate or invalidate the assumptions behind those beliefs.

In everyday conversation it is probably unrealistic for us to expect people to qualify their statements by explicitly differentiating facts from beliefs. Obviously, people don't consistently state facts as facts or beliefs as beliefs; nor is this necessary. It is not the technical accuracy of a statement which is the primary issue. The most important considerations are that we (1) make these distinctions in our own minds before we speak and (2) solicit feedback from others to insure that they haven't misinterpreted a belief as a fact.

In distinguishing between facts and beliefs, another area which requires special attention is our orientation toward time as represented by the past, present, and future. With respect to the past, we can know with absolute certainty that various events took place ("I graduated from college"). We frequently make the mistake, however, of talking about beliefs regarding the past as if they were facts ("I know my way was best even though nobody else agreed"). If we correct for this kind of distortion, it is frequently accurate to say "I know" when referring to the past.

In contrast, you can never know with absolute certainty what will happen one second from now, next week, or next year. For instance, you can know for a fact that you're in your car right now, but you can't know for certain that you will arrive at work safely. There are simply too many factors over which you have no control. Your car could go out of control, someone else might run into you, you could have a heart attack, there could be an earthquake, and so on. More likely than not, you don't think about any of these possibilities. You get in your car and drive to work as if the only possible outcome were to arrive safely. And you have no reason to doubt this since you have never had an accident. Regardless of your previous driving record, there is no way you can know for a fact what will happen this time or any future time you drive to work. Yet you continue driving anyway, with little thought of the perils which await you.

Relating this process directly to your work as a manager, have you ever had an employee who was so consistent in her work that you could always depend on her to perform at her best? If so, it is likely that you have failed to meet some crucial deadline due to an unexpected slump in her performance. When you are around the same people most of the time, it is easy to assume that what was a fact in the past will be a fact in the future. For this reason, it frequently takes a conscious effort to separate facts from beliefs.

Through A Belief Darkly

Another important factor to consider is that people have the ability to formulate a type of belief which is called a "conclusion". A *conclusion*, which can be formed from one or more facts or beliefs, is a judgment made after thinking about an issue or concern. Conclusions can be made regarding oneself, other people, or any aspect of life. Like other beliefs, conclusions are used to interpret experiences or predict what will happen in the future. In the example about driving, you probably combined some facts and beliefs to form a conclusion that it is safe to take your car to work. Based on this conclusion, you predict that you will arrive at work safely this morning. A *prediction*, of course, can never be anything more than a belief about what is going to happen, even though based on both solid evidence from the past and thorough consideration of relevant factors in the present. Since the future is always unknown, the only way you can decide how to act is to rely on beliefs (predictions).

This doesn't imply that people have the same degree of confidence in all their beliefs. Beliefs which are consistently successful in interpreting present experiences or predicting the future will be held with more confidence and be more resistant to change than beliefs which are inconsistent at these tasks. Less reliable beliefs are more readily subjected to scrutiny and change as people attempt to become more successful at meeting their needs. The conclusion you have reached about your ability to drive to work safely will probably be held with considerable confidence and resist change, unless you have an accident. Then you may decide to reassess your beliefs about driving, and taking the bus may not seem as inconvenient as it did yesterday.

Most adults have many beliefs held with such high confidence that they are completely taken for granted. This is when people are most susceptible to mistaking their beliefs for facts. Moreover, people frequently behave as though their beliefs and reality are identical. In one sense there is some truth to this. People's beliefs are their way of understanding themselves, other people, and the world around them. In essence, their beliefs become reality for them. It is indeed a mistake, however, when people conclude that their beliefs represent the one and only concept of reality. To paraphrase, it is like looking at life "through a belief darkly."

People who act on beliefs as if they were facts, or who assume that everyone sees the world the same way they do, can expect surprises in life. But no wonder that people reach these conclusions, since we often fail to teach individuals how the process of believing works. People rarely enter a new situation and systematically evaluate all possible interpretations before formulating a belief, and only then develop a course of action. It is more typical for people to quickly formulate a belief and act on it as if that belief were the only one possible. Furthermore, they frequently are unwilling or unable to assess the results of their behavior and relate this data back to original beliefs. This latter process creates situations in which people retain many mistaken, inaccurate, and incomplete beliefs which greatly inhibit behavior.

Managing in a Tower of Babel

No two people have the same set of beliefs. People not only have different experiences, but, more important, they attach different interpretations to the same experience. One person's success is another person's failure. On a more common level, how many times have you said or done something as a supervisor that you thought was interpreted by your employees as you intended, only to find later that it was completely misinterpreted? And most of you have probably had the experience of giving clear and specific instructions, and later found your employees dutifully doing something different. Sometimes these situations come to your attention so that you can correct them, but they frequently remain beyond your awareness and never get interpreted properly. You have probably wished you could get inside your employees' heads to see exactly how they interpret what you say. Since this is impossible, it underscores the importance of doing everything you can to make sure that employees accurately understand.

Since no two people have the same beliefs, they will define reality in different ways. And you thought you could easily master the challenges of management. Here you are with production goals and deadlines, and everyone on your staff is walking around with a different concept of reality. As if this wasn't enough, they usually don't even know that their concepts of reality differ. This sounds like such a good theme for a science fiction novel because it is a case where fact is clearly stranger than fiction. The unfortunate fact is that this predicament exists in every organization in the world and may exist as long as humans survive. Are you sure you still want to be a manager?

You're probably wondering why we can't clarify all this confusion and increase production at the same time. That certainly is the goal, but there are a number of factors which slow the reduction of confusion. To begin with, it is difficult to test the validity of one's beliefs. There are, of course, some instances when it is relatively easy to see that a different belief would be preferable to the one you hold at present. If you believe money is an incentive for everyone, for example, experience might show you that there are exceptions to this. Unfortunately, there are many areas of life which do not readily lend themselves to this kind of validation or invalidation. For instance, how do you prove your belief that work is intrinsically good? It is possible that future research could find a relationship between work and some dreaded disease; until then everyone is entitled to an opinion about the merits of working. All of us hold many beliefs which cannot be proven right or wrong. As a result, we assume they are correct and never question them. People make decisions based on these beliefs, but they aren't necessarily aware of the connection between beliefs and subsequent action. In fact, such awareness is the exception and not the rule. Behavior patterns become so habitual that people don't see that beliefs are guiding everything they do.

Although many beliefs cannot be proven correct or incorrect, they can be evaluated in terms of the consequences they have for one's life. It is possible for a person to assess the merits of beliefs by determining whether they have facilitative or inhibiting consequences. This process, known as "reality testing," can help people rid themselves of beliefs which have negative results and establish interpretations which foster positive outcomes. Unfortunately, most people never learn how to systematically evaluate the outcome of beliefs and use this information to determine whether beliefs should be modified. Instead, they continue to assume that their current beliefs and reality are the same and to act on those beliefs without question.

This brings me to an important consideration about beliefs: People want to believe that their beliefs are correct. In other words, people have a vested interest in the beliefs they hold. For many people, questioning their beliefs is tantamount to questioning their ability to accurately understand reality. This is usually an anxiety-provoking experience, one which people try to avoid. Therefore, when beliefs are challenged or contradicted by new evidence, many people become defensive and refuse to acknowledge, either to themselves or others, that their current beliefs may be inaccurate. Such expressions as "Don't confuse me with the facts" note the stubbornness with which people hold onto beliefs in spite of contrary evidence.

To understand why people act this way, it should be remembered that they are simultaneously motivated to improve themselves and to maintain the integrity of their personalities. If a person feels threatened, protecting the personality takes precedence over other motives. For example, some people form the conclusion that their abilities are only "average." It is possible for them to become very comfortable with this conclusion if it means that fewer demands will be placed on them. As such, an opportunity to excel at something could be regarded as threatening. In situations involving either real or imagined threat to personality, beliefs become very resistant to change. Change usually becomes a more viable option when people feel safe enough to relax their defenses. This is important to keep in mind when you manage employees. Generally, nonthreatening approaches are more effective in fostering change than threatening ones. There are exceptions. At gun-point most people will do what you ask, but an environment of physical and psychological safety is much more conducive to change. If the right conditions are present, positive change can occur more frequently than we sometimes believe. (Chapter 5 shows how to establish the necessary conditions to encourage positive change.)

While it is true that people formulate beliefs to account for all their experiences, some beliefs have more impact than others. For our purposes as supervisors and managers, the most important beliefs are those which people hold about themselves, other people (employees), and where they work. These three major categories of beliefs will be discussed separately.

Beliefs About Self

Everyone must formulate beliefs that answer fundamental questions like "Who am I?," "What are my capabilities?," "How am I different from others?," and "What are my unique qualities?" Seeking answers to these and other important questions about the self is a lifelong process. A child's beliefs about self are much more tentative than those of an adult, but even an adult's beliefs are not immune to change. Adults continue to have new experiences, regardless of age, so their beliefs about self are always subject to change. The fluidity of these beliefs is one of the major reasons why you should feel encouraged about the possibility of bringing about change in others.

To a great extent, the fulfillment people achieve in life depends upon whether their self-concept is basically positive or negative. It would be incongruous to find people with a negative self-concept spending a lot of time and energy developing their potential. They simply don't see any potential to develop. One's experiences and interpretations of those experiences are crucial in determining the nature of the self-concept. People cannot simply coax themselves into positive beliefs about self which are independent of their experiences. Those who attempt to do this are regarded as being "out of touch with reality." Instead, a set of positive beliefs about the self must be won in the real world, with successful experiences. Personal fulfillment must be related to actual achievements in order to be "real." Providing someone with an opportunity to have what they regard as a success in an area which has been characterized by failure may help them change beliefs about what they can do. This, in turn, may enable them to achieve something which previously would have been considered impossible.

For our purposes, perhaps the most important subcategory of beliefs within the self-concept is the view that people have regarding their competence. Beliefs regarding one's competence or incompetence are a major factor in determining whether the self-concept will be positive or negative. Like other beliefs about the self, competence must be demonstrated in the real world. It is extremely rare for people to develop an accurate belief that they are competent without external validation from others. For example, it would be hard to see how I could consider myself an effective consultant if no one hired me. At some point, the concept I have about my competence must correlate with the views of other people. We have little patience with people who profess to be competent, but prove in actual practice to be incompetent. Our attention is drawn to people who do this because everyone is implicitly expected to hold views of themselves which stand up under scrutiny.

While it is important for a correlation to exist between our view of our competence and the way others view it, it is also important that we not be totally dependent upon the views of others. Children and some adults have a concept of their competence which is almost completely dependent upon what others think of them. As a result, they constantly seek approval and feel either up or down depending upon feedback they receive from others. It is difficult for these people to think about themselves independent of others' opinions. Before they choose what to do, they try to determine whether or not it would meet others' approval. Choices which might not be accepted by others are abandoned in favor of safer alternatives. If these people could verbalize this process, they would be saying, "I am what others want me to be."

The other extreme consists of people who maintain beliefs about their competence that are entirely independent of the views of others. There are two variations of this pattern. The first is the person who feels competent even though others don't share this opinion, and the second is the person who claims to be incompetent in spite of evidence to the contrary. Verbalizing these processes would lead to a statement like, "I am what I am regardless of what others think."

The truth is somewhere in between these extremes. A belief in one's competence usually must have external validation from others to be sound. At the same time, however, the belief must be independent enough from the views of others to allow creativity and to prevent people from changing back and forth between feeling competent and incompetent, depending upon what somebody else says. Through time, people usually gain enough external validation to conclude that they are competent. This conclusion can then help them retain a belief in their competence in spite of occasional criticism from others. The more your employees hold positive self-concepts, the more likely it is that they will participate positively in change. You have a role in this.

Beliefs About Others

Next to beliefs about self, nothing is so central to fulfillment and productivity than the nature of our beliefs about others. It is virtually impossible to get most of our survival and growth needs met without other prople. Most of our day-to-day behavior consists of meeting the needs of others and others meeting our needs. In a work setting it means working *together* to get things done. When this process is functioning smoothly, it results in harmonious interdependence between people. The lack of such interdependence, however, normally leads to conflict of some kind. Beliefs about others are key ingredients in determining whether harmony or conflict is the outcome of interpersonal relationships. This becomes particularly clear when we probe beneath the surface of both effective and ineffective work groups.

People can form conclusions about individuals, specific groups of people (women, blacks, management), or all humanity. The capacity to establish conclusions about others can be an asset or a liability depending upon how it is used. Conclusions are only as good as the specific facts or beliefs that found them. If continually assessed for accuracy and modified to account for new information, conclusions can help people know what to expect from each other. For example, a manager may conclude that although there are exceptions, most employees sincerely want to do the best job they can. This conclusion may improve the ability of the manager to relate constructively to employees. It may also improve employee response.

People can use conclusions in ways which have a negative impact on relationships. For example, when people meet for the first time they form impressions of each other. The primary purpose of these impressions is to help people decide if the other person can be trusted. There is nothing wrong with this process, per se. In fact, the need for safety probably dictates that people resolve this issue of trust before moving ahead with other matters. The problem occurs when people have what they define as an intuitive hunch which is used to form a conclusion that someone can or cannot be trusted. People could avoid making unnecessary mistakes by attempting to identify any relevant facts and beliefs that would either validate or invalidate these hunches before forming conclusions regarding how much others can be trusted.

A stereotype is another example of a conclusion which tends to have a negative effect on relationships. A *stereotype* is a set of beliefs about the characteristics or behavior of a definable group of people, such as a minority group.

When representatives of a particular group are encountered, it is assumed that they possess all the characteristics which are attributed to the entire group. This greatly diminishes the likelihood that people will be able to relate to others as unique individuals.

Sometimes people establish conclusions about others under one set of circumstances and make the mistake of assuming that they will be valid under different circumstances. At other times people retain conclusions valid in the past, even though changes make the conclusions inadequate for relating to people in the present, and do not allow others to change.

Take the statement, "People will never appreciate what I do for this organization." Frequently, when people make a prediction like this it is based on a conclusion formulated in the past. The conclusion may be backed by substantial evidence; however, the assumption that it will always be true may prevent people from noticing others' new behavior which could modify the conclusion. Unfortunately, it is difficult to do anything about beliefs like this, because people seldom reveal them.

It is important to recognize changes in other people so that we can make any necessary adjustments in our conclusions about them. In addition, we must be aware of their potential for change before we can help them develop their fullest capabilities.

Beliefs About the Work Environment

In addition to beliefs about self and others, beliefs about the work environment are important in determining whether or not people will perform well. This includes beliefs about such working conditions as wages, breaks, fringe benefits, and physical surroundings in which they work. Employees may believe, for example, that they are competent and that other people are basically trustworthy, but also believe that the physical conditions under which they work are unacceptable. As a result of the latter beliefs, their desire to do their best may be impaired. A change in their beliefs or in physical conditions would have to take place before improved performance could reasonably be expected.

Some factors regarding the work place lend themselves to change while others do not. When factors cannot be changed, getting people to accept the inevitable has always been and will continue to be difficult. Frequently the problem is not with the work environment itself, but with the expectations people have. Working conditions are a case in point. It doesn't take long for privileges to be converted into rights in the minds of employees. People are reluctant to give up "rights," even if their expectations are unreasonable.

Occasionally, managers are faced with employees who would complain no matter how much was done to accommodate their wishes. They believe that nothing is ever good enough and take every opportunity to make this clear to you and everyone else. Although employees like this are not common, they can certainly make the job of a manager difficult and even miserable. Sometimes it is possible to work with them to change their beliefs. At other times nothing may work, and the only options may be to accept them as they are or terminate them.

You Value What Meets Your Needs 3

A *value* is a belief of a very special type. For this discussion I want to clearly differentiate values from other types of beliefs. The beliefs we talked about in chapter 2 have to do with our conceptions about what is correct and incorrect (descriptive beliefs) and what is good or bad (evaluative beliefs). On the other hand, *values represent our conceptions about what is worth pursuing in life.* There is a strong relationship between needs and the development and use of values. When people feel a need they must decide whether or not to satisfy it. Some survival needs, such as those for food, water, sleep, and shelter must be pursued to maintain life. In contrast, people may or may not pursue such growth needs as love, belonging, approval from others, self-regard, and creativity. The rich diversity of human activity results primarily from decisions people make about which needs they will try to fulfill.

As people determine which needs to satisfy, they rely heavily upon descriptive and evaluative beliefs. In fact, these beliefs supply the interpretations and conclusions upon which values are built. Although descriptive and evaluative beliefs greatly influence our actions, they may or may not affect behavior in any given situation. By definition, however, values must be related to what we do. The reason for this is that *descriptive and evaluative beliefs reflect what we think, while values stand for what we want.* Sometimes it is difficult to distinguish between an evaluative belief and a value. To make this distinction, consider that it is possible to believe something is good without doing anything about it. For example, you can believe management by objectives is very effective but not bother to use it with your employees. It is inconsistent, however, to say that you hold a value unless that value is reflected in your behavior.

Thus, values are beliefs which have been elevated to the status of guiding purposes for one's life. In *The Nature of Human Values*, Milton Rokeach asserts that "values are the cognitive representations and transformations of needs" (1973, p. 20). Once a value is established, we choose behavior which will allow us to serve that value, and ultimately the need it represents. As such, values function as motives for our behavior. *Whether we are aware of it or not, every behavior we engage in is motivated by one or more values.*

The role of values as purposes needs to be underscored. One of the unique aspects about human beings is that they are capable of selecting their own purposes. If this were not true, it would be difficult to maintain that people are responsible for their decisions. People don't simply act on instinct. They decide what is the best way to go about meeting their needs and then they act. In this process of trying out behavior to meet needs values are formed.

To demonstrate the connection between needs and values, let's say that a man has a need for approval from others. Over the years he has behaved in a variety of ways to gain that approval. Some behavior has been successful while other behavior has not. One form of behavior proven particularly useful to him in meeting this need is showing others how they can perform more effectively. The appreciation which others express to him is a great source of personal satisfaction. As a result, he develops a value for helping other workers and chooses to do this whenever possible.

Two Kinds of Values

Rokeach uses the terms *instrumental value* to refer to a desirable mode of conduct and *terminal value* when discussing a desirable end. Although my thinking has been greatly influenced by Rokeach, I prefer to use the terms *process* and *outcome* instead of *instrumental* and *terminal*. *Process values* have to do with such things as being ambitious, courageous, friendly, helpful, honest, logical, and with such activities as working with one's hands or being outdoors. In contrast, *outcome values* are concerned with such things as equality, family security, freedom, happiness, riches, self-respect, and friendship. To say that people have a process value indicates that they believe it is desirable to engage in the process of being helpful, friendly, working with their hands, and so on. To say that people have an outcome value indicates that they believe it is desirable to strive for the attainment of equality, self-respect, riches, and so on.

I agree with Rokeach when he says that there is not necessarily a relationship between what he calls instrumental values and terminal values. Unfortunately, his use of the term *means* to describe instrumental values implies that they are subservient to some other more important end. This is precisely why I prefer the term *process value*. To say, for example, that someone values the process of being honest does not imply that this value is a means to some other end. Valuing being honest may or may not be associated with other process or outcome values. It is quite possible to hold a process value for being honest which serves as its own end.

Another reason I prefer the term *process value* is that, unlike Rokeach's concept of instrumental value, it is not limited to describing certain desirable modes of conduct. To me, the phrase "mode of conduct" implies some kind of observable behavior. In contrast, *process value* is more flexible because it not only allows us to talk about values that result in observable behavior, but also values for thinking, reflection, contemplation, meditation, and other mental activities that cannot be directly observed.

I'd like to comment about outcome values. Usually, when the term *outcome* is used we tend to think of a specific or short-term result. In one sense, all values have short-term outcomes in that they guide behavior toward fulfilling needs. When I use *outcome value*, however, I am referring to a *final* outcome that people believe is worth pursuing, even though it can never be completely attained. For example, you may value wisdom and spend much of your time in activity related to this value. Nevertheless, even if the amount of knowledge you gain increased tremendously throughout your life, you would still be unable to achieve perfect wisdom.

Value Systems

Another phenomenon we need to consider is that people organize their values into *value systems*. Within these systems, both process and outcome values are structured into a fairly stable hierarchy of relative importance. People's values have differing effects on their behavior and their emotions depending upon their dominance or priority within the system.

As with beliefs, values stimulate the physiological responses we refer to as feelings or emotions. We are happy and exhilarated when we can pursue our values, angry and frustrated when we cannot. We like people who hold similar values and often dislike those who do not. The intensity of these emotions will vary in relation to the importance particular values have for us — to their relative positions in our value systems.

Similarly, people spend as much time as they can in activities that serve their dominant values. This is not to imply that the values in one's value system are static and unchangeable. Value systems are characterized by both stability and flexibility. The relative dominance of values shifts as people go through the routine of daily life. For example, during the day people may pursue a value for achievement and then in the evening pursue values for recreation and friendship.

Furthermore, just because people establish a value does not mean that they are stuck with it forever. People are capable of changing their values if they elect to do so. New experiences may lead to the development of new values. Also, values regarded as important earlier may be discarded or reduced in priority as people seek to fulfill different needs. (In Part II, I will have more to say about how values change and about how they resist change.)

You Do What You Value

Values all tend to sound good and noble on the surface. Consequently, people can verbally state that they have a value, even though that value has no impact on their behavior. There are a variety of reasons people do this (see chapter 6). People cannot be said to have a value unless that value guides the choices they make in meeting their needs.

As with beliefs, our primary interests are with three categories of values—those which pertain to the self, others, and the work environment. These categories will be discussed separately.

Values Pertaining to the Self

These values are concerned with such processes as being ambitious, courageous, creative, playful, and active, and such outcomes as achievement, happiness, self-understanding, wisdom, and power. A person may embrace a combination of these and other values which focus on the self, but time limits how much all of them can be pursued. Therefore, people must decide to place a higher priority on some values rather than others. The direction people take in life and how much they realize their potential depends largely upon the priority assigned to various personal values.

Perhaps an example will show how pursuing one value affects the attention which can be devoted to other values. To prepare for careers in a professional field like medicine or law, people are required to successfully complete a rigorous educational program. People would need to place high priority on achievement and postpone or forego other values, such as comfort, to obtain the necessary education. Someone else with equal ability may not be willing to make the sacrifices required to earn a degree in one of these fields because higher priority is placed on other values.

The personal values of employees will have a great effect on their behavior at work. For example, some employees place a high value on being capable at work, while others are satisfied to just get by because their values are elsewhere. Although there are exceptions, employees are usually more productive and reliable if they value the quality of their work. Initiating action designed to increase the extent to which people value being capable can be one of the most effective ways to achieve the goals of an organization.

Values Pertaining to Others

People's lives are also greatly affected by the values they have regarding others. Since people are interdependent in meeting their needs, it is important for them to take into consideration both what they want for themselves and what they want for others. Process values for being cooperative, helpful, and forgiving, and outcome values for equality and friendship can foster personal relationships, while a lack of such values may greatly inhibit the desire and ability to get along with others. Personal goals which lead to very self-centered behavior may also have negative effects on other people. In addition, it is possible for people to do so much for others that they neglect their own development. The most functional arrangement would seem to be a balance between values which focus on self and others, permitting people to both pursue their own values and help others do the same.

An infant has no regard for the needs of others. It is only when a person starts to recognize a need for belonging and respect that taking others into consideration becomes valued. Most people learn that helping others meet their needs makes them feel good about themselves, which reinforces this kind of behavior. It should be noted that there is no such thing as altruistic motivation. Whether we are aware of it or not, everything we do stems from one or more of our own needs. Some people mistakenly view their behavior as being altruistic, while others feel guilty when they think it isn't. Both perspectives are incorrect. The fact that all our behavior is motivated by needs merely points out that we are human. The key variable we have some control over is how the choices we make in meeting our needs affect other people.

Values Pertaining to the Work Environment

In addition to values which focus on oneself and others, people also formulate values for certain kinds of job assignments and working conditions. There are many times when it is necessary for the manager to be aware of differences in such values in order to work effectively with employees. Some employees, for example, value the process of working outdoors while others value working indoors. Not recognizing these differences might cause problems for the manager which could be prevented. The same is true of specific tasks performed by an employee. Two employees of equal ability may be assigned to the same type of work. One person might really value the process of engaging in that particular work, while the other might prefer to do anything but the work assigned. People try to spend as much time as possible in valued activities. They will resent having to endure activities which are not related to their values. If you want to get the most out of your employees, assign them to activities which allow them to pursue their values, and try to eliminate activities which interfere with this.

Another example which directly relates to your job as a manager is the task of dealing with paperwork. Some managers loathe paperwork, while others enjoy it and take great pride in the way they handle routine administrative chores. Those in the first category will endure the paperwork assignments or delegate them to others, whereas those in the second group will spend as much time in the company of paper as possible. These differences will greatly affect both how people feel about their jobs and their daily performance.

The Relationship 4 Between Values and Beliefs

In the previous chapters, I discussed how people establish values and beliefs to meet their various needs, and talked about the types of values and beliefs most relevant to managers. I concluded that what we actually do is greatly influenced by what we believe and what we value. Sometimes it is possible to predict behavior by knowing a person's values and beliefs, but this is not always the case. Since values and beliefs are mental constructs that we cannot get inside a person's head to "see," they must be inferred from what that person says or does. This task would be easier if there were a clear relationship between values and beliefs on the one hand, and behavior on the other. Unfortunately, the processes involved are not simple because values and beliefs influence not only behavior but one another. That is, values affect other values, beliefs affect other beliefs, and values and beliefs affect each other.

There is a constant give-and-take between values and beliefs which complicates the task of trying to accurately predict or understand behavior. Through a combination of observing and talking to people, it is possible to see how this give-and-take affects behavior. There are times, however, when the influence of values and beliefs on one another is so subtle that the connection between this process and a person's subsequent behavior is difficult to recognize. To effectively deal with resistance it is important to understand these relationships as fully as possible. I have identified eight major ways that values and beliefs influence each other (see figure 1).

Present Values Can Affect the Development of New Values

Once people formulate a value, that value can either promote or interfere with the establishment of new values. For example, people may decide to enroll in an apprenticeship program because they value money but develop values for learning and quality workmanship in their program experience. These new values may open up a whole new world which has a direct impact on the goals these people feel are worth achieving in life.

Sometimes, however, existing values can have the opposite effect. For example, an employee may place such high value on independence that it interferes with developing a value for cooperation. As a result, the employee could have difficulty working on a project which required a team approach. Salespeople who have worked in the field on commission often have problems when promoted to the marketing staff.

Present Values Can Have an Impact on Other Present Values

It is possible for values which are already established to either promote or interfere with other established values.

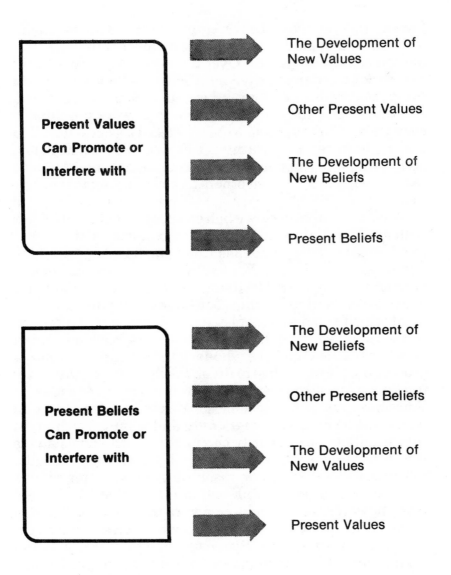

Fig. 1   The Effects of Values and Beliefs on Each Other

For example, suppose that an employee in your department, Cathy Wagner, places a high value on present performance and on self-improvement. Over time you have noticed that her work procedures are not as efficient as they could be. In the past, certain employees became defensive when you mentioned that they could improve their work procedures, even though they wanted to be as effective as possible. You realize, however, that Cathy is less likely to become defensive, because she not only wants to be capable now but also regards suggestions from others as a useful way to improve herself.

A value conflict occurs when one present value interferes with another. Value conflicts can be experienced with varying degrees of intensity depending upon how important the values are to a person. For example, let's say that one of your employees, Mark Goodwin, possesses strong values for achievement and friendship. You have given him an assignment which you need completed by tomorrow if at all possible. Without realizing it, you have put Mark in a bind. He is a very ambitious employee who is working hard to secure a promotion. He would like to finish the assignment this evening and give you the results tomorrow morning. At the same time, however, some very close friends he hasn't seen in years will be in town tonight only and want to see him. In this situation, he obviously can't act on both values and is forced to make a difficult decision between them. Ideally, dilemmas like this can be resolved by, say, acting on one value now and postponing action on another. As a manager, however, you should be aware that you will have to make decisions or propose choices which create value conflicts for your employees. By recognizing these conflicts and taking steps to help employees resolve them, you will be freeing them for more effective performance.

Present Values Can Affect the Development of New Beliefs

Once a person forms a value, that value can either promote or interfere with establishing new beliefs. For example, let's assume that you value equality but are not aware of how much women and minorities are underrepresented in the work force. Your organization recently implemented a new affirmative action plan with definite goals and timetables for hiring and promoting women and minorities. After reviewing a demographic study of current employees, you develop a belief that the affirmative action plan is needed. In all probability, your value for equality helped you develop this belief.

At the same time, you are aware that some of your colleagues who highly value self-reliance have been against hiring and promotion guidelines which give any advantage to one group over another. In this instance, it is possible that their value for self-reliance could interfere with the development of a favorable belief regarding the affirmative action plan.

Present Values Can Have an Impact on Present Beliefs

Established values can either promote or interfere with established beliefs. Let's suppose, for example, that you place a high value on job security. You have just been promoted to a management position and it is very important that you succeed in your new job. There are several other managers who report to the same vice president. On your first day at work, some of your colleagues tell you that the boss is a moody person who has a difficult time getting along with people. While this information is somewhat disconcerting, you believe that with sufficient effort you can establish an effective working relationship with anybody.

Since your value and belief are compatible, it is likely that you will be able to develop an adequate way of relating to the boss.

There are times, however, when a value interferes with the ability to act on a belief. For example, let's say you were made aware of the possibility that certain unnamed employees are receiving kickbacks for showing favoritism to certain contractors. Following this, you held a meeting of all employees in your department and indicated that you wanted any act of dishonesty to be reported. Unknown to you, this puts Eric Simpson, one of your employees, in a dilemma. He is aware of some employees who have received kickbacks and believes that dishonesty of this kind is wrong. However, he values loyalty to his fellow workers. As a result, he decides not to reveal the names of guilty employees. In this case, Eric's value for loyalty interferes with his acting on the belief that dishonesty is wrong.

Present Beliefs Can Affect the Development of New Beliefs

Beliefs which you currently hold can either facilitate or inhibit establishing new beliefs. For example, if you believe that people are basically conscientious this might help you establish a belief that employees should be given the benefit of the doubt if they occasionally report to work late. If, however, you believe people are basically undependable, it is doubtful that you would develop the belief that occasional tardiness should be permitted.

Present Beliefs Can Have an Impact on Other Present Beliefs

Established beliefs can promote or interfere with other established beliefs. There may be occasions, for example, when you need employees to volunteer for special assignments which will require them to function with minimum supervision. Employees will be more likely to volunteer for these assignments if they not only believe they are competent, but also believe they can succeed in new situations. Those employees who hold the former belief but not the latter may be unwilling to volunteer.

It is also possible for conflicts to develop among one's beliefs. For example, let's say that the management of your company tried to negotiate a new contract with the labor union. Management made an offer but it was less than the union wanted. As a result, the union decided to go on strike. This put one of your employees, Ted Logan, in a difficult situation. Ted believes that the offer made by management is generous, but also believes that belonging to the union is in the best interest of workers. He must decide whether to go on strike or remain on the job. After giving the matter considerable thought, Ted went along with the decision of the union. Thus, his belief about the importance of belonging to the union prevailed over his belief that the offer made by management was a good one.

Present Beliefs Can Affect the Development of New Values

Current beliefs can either promote or interfere with the development of new values. One of your employees, Martha Anderson, believed that she had considerable potential for advancement, perhaps in computer programming. Her experience had been limited to technical jobs in accounting. Because of your belief that she has management potential you decide to talk with her about her career aspirations. When you asked her if she ever thought about going into management, she indicated that she hadn't thought about it very much but mentioned interest in computer programming. The following week you asked Martha to fill in for her supervisor who was out due to illness. As a result of this experience, she developed a value for leadership and began preparing for a career in management. In this situation, the fact that Martha believed in her potential for advancement helped her form a value for becoming a leader.

Current beliefs can also prevent the establishment of new values. For example, John Crosby has worked as an assistant manager at his father's clothing store for several years. His father promises to promote him to general manager when the current general manager retires in five years. John has a bachelor's in business and performs duties which are far below his capability. In fact, John has enough knowledge and skill right now to own and operate his own store. The problem is that John believes he would be letting his father down if he didn't stay and eventually manage the family store. As a result, John does not place much importance on self-reliance, independence, and other values which could motivate him to open his own store. The thought never occurs to John that he could utilize more talent and be more successful if he went out on his own. To do this would go against his beliefs.

Present Beliefs Can Have an Impact on Present Values

Established beliefs can either promote or interfere with established values. If you believe you can trust your employees and if you value openness, you might be willing to share confidential information with them on a regular basis. Thus, your belief fosters actions associated with the value you have for openness. On the other hand, you might be suspicious of your employees and decide to keep all confidential information to yourself. This is a case where your belief clearly interferes with actions related to the value you place on openness.

There are, of course, other alternatives available. For example, you might confront the group with your suspicions in an effort to reestablish trust, or you could threaten to fire anyone caught revealing confidential information. Another option would be to lower the importance that openness has for you as a value. Any alternative you choose will have an impact on the relationship you have with your employees, and the outcome of this impact will tend to be either positive or negative.

I've tried to show that a very fluid and dynamic relationship exists between one's values and beliefs. In each example, I described specific cases in which a value was affecting a belief, a belief affecting another belief, or a belief affecting a value. My purpose was to provide a mental exercise designed to increase the extent to which you could visualize the effects that values and beliefs have on each other and on behavior. In real life situations, these relationships are seldom this clear-cut. Sometimes it is very difficult to determine whether a value is affecting a belief or vice versa. At other times, a chain reaction takes place where the influence of values and beliefs on one another switches back and forth. Like the chicken and the egg, in many instances it is simply impossible to tell what came first, the value or the belief. It is *possible*, however, to be more effective in dealing with resistance as you develop a better feel for values and beliefs, and their influence on each other.

PART II

Understanding Resistance

Change and **5** *Resistance*

People Can Change

In Part I, I talked about how people get to be the way they are. I indicated that people think before they act and discussed the significant role played by facts, beliefs, and values in the thinking process. Now I'd like to switch gears and talk about how people become different from what they are — *how they change*. Specifically, I will focus on the change process as it relates to individuals and small work groups rather than on large-scale changes in organizational structure and function.

People are capable of changing the way they think and the way they act. It is possible for people to change the way they act, at least temporarily, without changing their thinking. It appears, however, that more complete and lasting behavior changes require a change in thinking. Since thinking depends to a large extent on the specific facts, beliefs, and values that people have established, a change in any of these leads most surely to a change in behavior. When people use the expression "I changed my mind," they mean they have found new facts or modified a belief or value. Although change in one or more facts, beliefs, and values usually precedes change in behavior, this is not always the case. Sometimes a chain reaction occurs where a change in a belief leads to a change in a behavior, which in turn leads to a change in another belief or value. Noting this "new thinking," let's examine more closely the human phenomenon of change.

Human beings are the only inhabitants of this world capable of determining their own destiny. And of even greater significance, they can change that destiny if they so choose. Can you imagine a caterpillar deciding not to become a butterfly or a salmon electing not to return to the spawning grounds? These are instinctual responses over which the creature has no control. In one sense, animals have an easier time because they don't struggle over the ultimate meaning of life, whether they would find greater fulfillment in one endeavor (flying) as opposed to another (swimming), or whether they are achieving their potential. They simply reenact the same pattern which has shaped the behavior of their species for countless generations.

Human beings have the capacity to select purposes from a great many alternatives. We can decide who we are and what is worth striving for. After our choices are made, we mobilize our behavior to serve these choices. If one action doesn't work as anticipated, we can try another or abandon the goal in favor of something else. The human experience is characterized by a ceaseless process of evaluating, deciding, behaving, reevaluating, and redeciding.

As a result, we are constantly undergoing change. We aren't the same today as yesterday and won't be the same tomorrow. Most changes in our lives occur so gradually that we aren't aware of them. For example, your ability to write reports may slowly improve over a period of years without you realizing that your skill has increased tremendously. Usually we only focus our attention on the change process when the change represents a major departure from what we previously were. If you move to a new town and start a different job, the change and accompanying adjustment are the predominant focus of your attention. Such changes can be and often are the source of agony, ecstasy, or something in between. Whether large or small, good or bad, change is our constant companion throughout life.

It may seem somewhat unusual that in a book on resistance I am marveling over the ability of people to change. This isn't contradictory. If people were incapable of change, there wouldn't be much need for strategies dealing with resistance. Since people can change, it is possible to improve the quality of life of those working below their potential. It is crucial to bear in mind that any change, large or small, will make people different from what they were before. There is no such thing as a change with a neutral impact: people will be better or worse off because of it. Those of us who are instigators of change should never forget this. Because the responsibilities involved are great, it is our job to systematically evaluate the pros and cons of any proposed change, and choose courses of action that have the highest probability of improving the lives of those with whom we work.

How People Change

Now let's examine in greater detail just how change takes place. Young children spend most of their day trying to figure out the world around them. When they experience something for the first time, either curiosity or fear of the unknown motivates them to assign a meaning to the experience which will help them understand it. If this meaning helps the child relate to the experience, the anxiety dissipates and the child will continue to rely on this meaning whenever the experience recurs. If, however, the original meaning assigned to an experience does not help someone relate to it, fear will reappear and that person will be motivated to seek a better explanation. For example, a child may pick up a bug, experience no problems, and conclude that all bugs are safe to play with. When this same child picks up another bug and is bitten, the need for a better set of interpretations regarding bugs becomes apparent. In short, people learn from their experiences.

Although the above example is a simple one, the process involved represents how people come to understand the world and their place in it. It is necessary for us to accuately interpret our experiences in order to go about the task of meeting our needs. As a result, we are constantly involved in refining the interpretations we give experiences, as we attempt to fulfill needs more effectively. This give-and-take between our environment and ourselves is the essence of learning. Over years we gradually learn more and more, which requires us to either make modifications in our current values and beliefs, or integrate new values and beliefs into our present personality structure. The capacity of people to develop and refine values and beliefs is one of their most important attributes; without this, creative thought and inventiveness would be greatly limited and the ability to solve problems would be seriously impaired. People would not be able to adapt to new circumstances; they would be unable to change.

The most fundamental statement we can make about change is that it is absolutely essential for growth of any kind. This principle is just as true for intellectual and emotional growth as for physical development. No change, no growth; it's that simple. It is also true, however, that certain conditions increase a person's motivation to change.

Conditions Favorable to Change

First, people are more likely to change if their current values, beliefs, or behavior do not allow them to adequately meet their needs. Recall that needs beckon for fulfillment, and our values and beliefs guide actions designed to meet needs. If our values, beliefs, or behavior do not allow us to adequately meet our needs, we feel anxious and frustrated. One option that people have in situations like this is to allow the need to go unfulfilled. However, it is more common for people to adjust their values, beliefs, or behavior. For example, a man may have a need for companionship at work, but believe that no one would be interested in having him as a friend. In this situation, a belief interferes with the man's ability to meet his need. Since he came up with this belief in the first place, he isn't stuck with it; he can change it if he wants to. To change a belief of this kind, the man will probably have to be more assertive in developing relationships with others. Although this process will probably create some anxiety which stems from the belief he holds about himself, trying new behavior in an effort to make friends is his best bet for changing the belief and ultimately meeting his need.

Second, people are usually more willing to change a value, belief, or behavior if they believe the change will help them more in meeting their needs. The problem with this, of course, is the impossibility of knowing the outcome of a change in advance. Some people want a guarantee that the change will lead to positive results, while others figure that they have nothing to lose and everything to gain. The first group will be reluctant to change, even though their current values, beliefs, and behavior prevent them from meeting some needs. They conclude that it is safer to stick with the known than to risk the unknown. By contrast, those in the second group will probably exhibit a greater willingness to change, increasing their chances of fulfilling unmet needs.

Third, people are more likely to change if the change is voluntary rather than coerced. Under the right conditions changes in behavior can be coerced ("You do it this way or you're fired"), but even here it is unlikely that the change will persist after the threat has been removed. If coercion is not a very effective way to change behavior, it is totally inept in changing values and beliefs. People might placate you by pretending to agree with your way of thinking or with your preferences, without any change taking place inside their heads.

And finally, people are much more likely to change if you actively involve them in the change process. This will help them want what you want. One of the basic principles of human behavior is that people support what they help create. If people are involved in bringing about a change, they will have an investment in it. The change will belong to everyone and not simply you.

The Phenomenon of Resistance

Perhaps the best way to begin our discussion of resistance is to compare it to readiness. *Readiness* is a state of mind reflecting willingness or receptiveness to change in the ways we think or behave, while *resistance* is a state of mind reflecting unwillingness or unreceptiveness to such changes. Readiness is manifested behaviorally by either active initiation of change or cooperation with it. In contrast, resistance manifests itself behaviorally by either active opposition to change or avoidance of it. In conversations, people frequently use the term *resistance* to refer to particular behavior. We hear that someone is resisting this or that. There is nothing wrong with this as long as we remember that resistance is also a state of mind indicating an unwillingness to change.

Readiness is not the opposite of resistance, since an absence of resistance doesn't necessarily mean that someone will be ready to change. Other variables, such as lack of information or an immediate need to attend to other matters, could interfere with readiness. Nevertheless, anything which causes resistance can be expected to undermine readiness in any given situation.

It would be useful to examine in general terms why people resist change. To begin with, life is the testing ground for forming values and beliefs. The bottom line for any value or belief is its ability to successfully guide behavior toward the fulfillment of needs. Values and beliefs successful at this task will be retained, while those which are unsuccessful will be modified or discarded. Initial values and beliefs that serve as effective guides to need-fulfilling behavior tend to influence the establishment of subsequent values and beliefs. A person's values and beliefs function much like a fraternity. New values and beliefs are admitted only if they are regarded as being compatible with existing members. In this way the personality of an individual evolves.

Any belief or value that has been previously successful in meeting needs will resist change. Of course, some beliefs and values will be more resistant to change than others. Those values and beliefs which have been consistently reinforced through experience, and which serve as the core around which other values and beliefs are added to personality will be most resistant to change. In contrast, values and beliefs which are less reliable in meeting needs will be more amenable to change. The degree of personal investment will be greater for the former values and beliefs as compared to the latter. People develop such a strong commitment to their most reliable values and beliefs that it is difficult for them to think of themselves apart from those values and beliefs. For practical purposes, they and their values and beliefs become synonymous.

The role of fear in creating resistance will be a major theme in this chapter. While fear is an emotion which alerts people to danger, the danger doesn't have to be real for fear to be activated. Imaginary danger can also cause fear. In either case, once fear surfaces, reducing the danger becomes a motive which takes precedence over other motives, such as fulfilling growth needs. Frequently, people experience fear when they believe one of their values or beliefs is being threatened. The fear then motivates them to protect and defend the value or belief in question. Of course the intensity of fear can vary from mild to extreme, depending upon the importance attached to a particular value or belief. People may only experience a small amount of fear if a relatively insignificant value or belief is threatened. In contrast, they may become tremendously afraid if one of their most cherished values or beliefs is attacked.

Another major factor which we need to consider in understanding resistance is the relationship between one's values, beliefs, and behavior. Since a person's values and beliefs become associated with one another and with certain patterns of behavior, changing even one value, belief, or behavior will have an impact on other values, beliefs, and behaviors. It is probably impossible to change one component part of the system without affecting other components. For example, if you teach your employees to do something they believed was beyond their capabilities, it is likely that this will lead to both changes in what they believe they can do and also what they want to do (values). Therefore, while it may sometimes appear simple enough for a person to change one value, belief, or behavior that is causing problems, related values, beliefs, and behaviors may complicate this or even prevent it from happening.

As noted in Part I, people's beliefs become their reality. Therefore, suggesting that a belief be altered is like asking them to modify their concept of reality to some extent. People are often reluctant to do this because they want to believe that their current interpretations of experience are accurate. It is crucial for you to understand that the vested interests people have regarding their present beliefs, which form reality as they see it, quite commonly interfere with their willingness to change, even when it could very likely have a positive effect on them. Vested interests of this kind, which can prevent people from objectively evaluating the potential benefits of any change, are one of the most common causes of resistance.

The Case Against Change and For Resistance

I don't want to give you the impression that change is always positive or that resistance is always negative. Change is neither inherently good nor bad. Although change can be evaluated by its consequences, it is impossible to know in advance if a change will turn out to be positive or negative. No change is neutral, however. After all the relevant factors have been considered, there are many instances when it is best not to make a change. For example, let's say that you have an assistant, Bill Arnold, who is not as efficient in his position as some other employee on your staff would be. However, Bill's rapport with those under his supervision is so strong that replacing him could have a very disruptive effect on the other employees. In this case, you determine that the costs of proposed change outweigh the benefits, and therefore decide not to replace Bill.

It is also necessary to recognize that every organization requires a certain amount of stability to function effectively. Constant change would lead to chaos. Organizations also need employees who want to continue doing what they are already good at. If managers spend too much time preparing employees for advancement (change), no one will be available to do work that needs to be done now — which could jeopardize the organization. Of course, it is very difficult to say when the amount of change is too much. One major challenge of any manager is locating the right balance between change and stability. Finding this balance lowers the probability that a manager will inadvertently encourage change that is dysfunctional for the organization.

Not only are there times when change is inadvisable, but there are other times when resistance is the best action. Unfortunately, when the word *resistance* is mentioned, we tend to ascribe negative connotations to it. This is a misconception. There are many times when resistance is the most effective response available. In France during World War II, for example, resistance was a positive term. It is also true that a healthy body *resists* illness, and this kind of resistance is not only adaptive but essential to our continued existence.

I have indicated that people are motivated both to protect the integrity of their personality and to grow. People need to have confidence in their values and beliefs before they feel secure enough to seek opportunities to grow. If people's values and beliefs provide them with constructive and effective ways of meeting needs, then it is adaptive and healthy for people to hold onto these values and beliefs, and resist change. Constructive values and beliefs bring continuity to one's life, which is necessary to meet needs in an orderly manner. Some changes could disrupt this process and cause a person to become disorganized and less effective. In these situations it is in a person's best interest to resist change.

The main point I want to make here is that there are times when resistance is a *problem* and times when it is a *solution*. Resistance is a *solution* when someone is trying to change you in a way which will either inhibit your development or cause you to become less effective. In this case my advice is resist, resist, resist. On the other hand, resistance is a *problem* when the proposed change would allow you to develop your potential more fully. Under these circumstances my advice is change, change, change. As you can see, I am biased in favor of change which enhances the quality of life for people. At the same time, I realize that change is not easy. In fact, it takes great courage to change. Every time someone is courageous enough to improve himself, the talent available for use by our organizations is increased.

We will now turn attention to the resistance matrix, to more fully explore the type of resistance labeled a problem.

The Resistance 6 Matrix

In everyday conversation, people often use the term *resistance* to indicate that others are against certain ways of thinking or behaving. Some expressions are limited to specifying whether resistance is present or absent. Thus, we hear statements like "There is resistance to using the new procedures" or "Some people will resist that idea while others will accept it." While such statements are common they aren't very imformative. They tell us nothing about why the resistance is there or what to do about it. Furthermore, they misrepresent the complex nature of resistance.

Some people go one step further and express the degree to which resistance is either present or absent. This is seen in such statements as "There is a great deal of resistance coming from certain employees" or "His resistance has decreased since last week." The intensity of resistance can be thought of as existing on a continuum which extends from none, at one end, to extreme, at the other end. If the intensity of resistance is low, it is often best to do nothing about it since it will often disappear as people become accustomed to the change. Drawing attention to it could have the effect of making it more intense or of prolonging it. Faced with intense resistance, you will, of course, have to do something about it. To specify the intensity of resistance in a particular instance, we can only rely upon a subjective estimate. As a result, people frequently disagree on just how much resistance is present. People need to discuss their estimates so that such disagreements can be identified and resolved, and appropriate actions planned.

Although the *intensity* of resistance is an important consideration, it is only one of three relevant variables which must be taken into account to fully describe and explain resistance in a specific situation. The other two variables are the *sources* and *focuses* of resistance. For our purposes, resistance can stem from four major sources, (i.e., facts, descriptive beliefs, evaluative beliefs, and values, and focus on oneself, other people, or the work environment). Taken together, these variables form a three-dimensional resistance matrix (see Figure 2).

The resistance matrix permits us to make highly meaningful statements about resistance. We can say, for example, that an employee demonstrates a small amount of resistance stemming from descriptive beliefs regarding other people (i.e., they are out to get him), and that another employee shows considerable resistance because of a certain value concerning the work environment (i.e., he wants to be able to talk with others while working). Once all relevant information regarding intensity, source, and focus have been identified for an actual case of resistance, your ability to develop an effective strategy to deal with it will be greatly enhanced.

At this point, I would like to provide a more thorough understanding of the resistance matrix. The variable of intensity was mentioned above, while the variable of focus was considered in Part I. Therefore, I won't repeat that

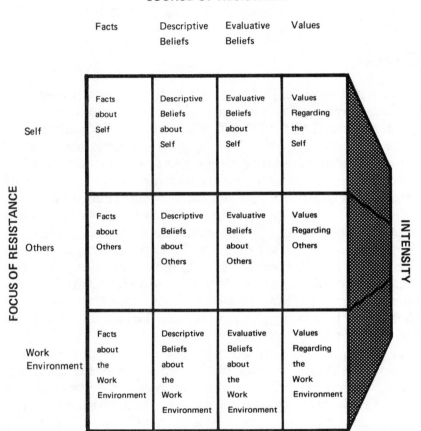

SOURCE OF RESISTANCE

Fig. 2 Resistance Matrix

information here. Instead, I will give an in-depth analysis of how the four major sources of resistance (facts, descriptive beliefs, evaluative beliefs, and values) can interfere with change.

Facts

Two issues are especially relevant in trying to determine the role played by facts in particular instances of resistance. First, you need to find out if you are actually dealing with facts, and second, you need to see how facts are used to foster resistance. In the first instance, absolute proof is needed for something to qualify as a fact. Anything short of this makes it a belief. So, the issue of evidence is key here. The second question, having to do with the way facts are used, is more tricky. When someone is resisting change, they may *selectively* bring up those facts which support their case. In other words, people may present some of the facts but not all the facts. People have a strong tendency to be aware of only those facts which increase the potency of their view. It is your job to make sure that all relevant facts are brought to the surface.

For example, a woman may not apply for a promotion because on three separate occasions she was turned down for advancement. The woman has received improved personnel ratings lately and scored high on a number of qualifying examinations for various positions. When she explains why she didn't apply for the promotion, she may present the former facts, but not the latter. You, of course, need to know as much as possible about her to understand why she is using facts selectively to resist change.

Facts are useful to people who want to escape or avoid something they are afraid of, because facts make such convincing rationalizations. The best way for people to get you off their backs is to bring up irrefutable evidence. this puts you in the position of having to deal with their evidence on their terms. Unfortunately, they can be so convincing that they end up preventing themselves from doing something which would enrich their career.

Facts, of course, are frequently highly relevant and useful in discussions where a decision is being made or a change proposed. You will be presenting facts in favor of your view, while others will be using facts to argue for their perspective. The problem is that facts can be used to shed light on a situation or they can be used to distort what's being discussed. If the interaction is conducted in a manner conducive to objective and rational consideration of all relevant facts, this can be a productive process.

When the level of resistance is intense, however, the ability of people to logically present and consider facts is reduced. If people are determined to have their own way, emotional and ego involvement in their views will interfere with their ability to present all facts and their willingness to listen to your facts. Intense emotion and reason don't mix. In an atmosphere charged with strong feelings, your ability to use logical persuasion to lower resistance will be reduced. Change through consensus requires a situation in which people don't feel threatened. Threat creates defensiveness, which increases the possibility that facts will be used to win a point rather than as the basis for an agreement in the best interest of all concerned.

Descriptive Beliefs

Up until now I have talked in general terms about how beliefs develop, and the role of beliefs in either fostering change or creating resistance. My objective has been to demonstrate that *any* belief is capable of promoting or interfering with one's efforts to meet needs and develop work-related personal, interpersonal, and technical skills. Therefore, I have deliberately avoided making a distinction between the relative advantages or disadvantages of various types of beliefs.

Unquestionably, some beliefs and some ways of using beliefs tend to be more inhibiting than others. For example, believing that all people think only of themselves will be more inhibiting than believing that many people think only of themselves. Believing that many people think only of themselves will be more inhibiting than believing that, while some are self-centered, most people are genuinely concerned about others. To further your understanding of beliefs, I am going to highlight various beliefs and believing processes which are especially significant in interfering with change.

Recall that *descriptive beliefs* are not facts but subjective interpretations which define for someone what is correct or incorrect. Essentially, a descriptive belief is a person's best guess regarding what something means or what is going to happen in the future. People are born problem solvers. They have a mental apparatus which permits them to attach meaning to very complex experiences, then use these meanings to direct their actions. Unfortunately, simply because people have a marvelous ability to formulate beliefs does not mean that those beliefs will necessarily be correct. People are just as capable of formulating inaccurate, incorrect, and mistaken beliefs.

Whether people formulate correct or inaccurate beliefs depends largely on what they regard as evidence. Generally, fewer errors are made when people rely on empirical evidence to test the validity of their beliefs. Empirical evidence is usually more effective than simply taking someone's word for it ("If you say so, then it must be true") or blindly assuming you are correct ("I can't prove it, but I know I'm right").

Of course, the empirical data necessary to validate or invalidate beliefs is more tangible and easier to gather in some situation than in others. For example, you can validate your belief that someone will always report to work on time by checking previous attendance records. On the other hand, your belief that instituting a system of management by objectives will improve productivity and lower the turnover rate may take months or years to validate. Nevertheless, it is possible to monitor behavioral changes over time and use the evidence to confirm or correct your belief. In fact, I maintain that empirical evidence can be used to assess the validity of any descriptive belief. The key is finding appropriate yardsticks against which to assess the particular beliefs which exist for any given situation.

This poses an important question: How much evidence is enough? Obviously, the answer will depend upon the specific belief. Beliefs that depend upon interpretations of behavior usually require more evidence than beliefs backed up by actual physical proof, or beliefs automatically confirmed when a predicted event occurs. It is very difficult to "prove" beliefs based on interpretations of behavior. Cases of complete proof or disproof are exceptional. Any behavior can be greatly influenced by factors unrelated to your belief or beyond your awareness. It is extremely hard to objectively examine behavior and separate those factors unrelated to the belief, and it is impossible to account for factors beyond your awareness.

Because of these factors, you should try to gather as much evidence as possible when assessing the validity of beliefs. There are, of course, limits to both cost and time. In your efforts to validate beliefs, it is often helpful to seek other opinions. In trying to make sense out of human behavior, other perspectives can be a real asset. Others may see things you are unaware of, which will allow a more accurate assessment of beliefs. The ideas of others can also provide clues to the kinds of modifications or refinements necessary to make beliefs more accurate.

Another major reason why you should seek input from others in validating beliefs is that your biases may prevent you from seeing all available evidence. Like most people, you probably want your beliefs to be correct and may consciously or unconsciously minimize or ignore contradictory evidence. Remember that people are capable of arguing in favor of any belief, even if the belief is wrong. Therefore, gaining consensus is a good way of keeping you from fooling yourself with your own beliefs. It is also a good way to help your employees test their beliefs.

Although the above issues are more pertinent to beliefs which depend upon interpretations of behavior, people are also capable of distorting evidence for beliefs backed by physical proof or historical precedence. For example, because your door opened for you nine times in a row is no guarantee that it will open the tenth time. At some point, your belief that the door will always open for you might be proven inaccurate. With beliefs in this category, be careful not to assume that you will always be correct because you were able to produce concrete evidence in support of your belief at one time. We all know people who stubbornly hold onto beliefs which were valid in the past but are no longer. A frequent reason is that people don't like to admit they're wrong. They would rather hold onto mistaken belief than objectively consider evidence to the contrary, even though this undermines their credibility. It is important for everyone to thoroughly scrutinize their beliefs and avoid maintaining those which they can't substantiate.

There are three types of believing processes that I would like to discuss briefly because of the frequency with which they result in mistaken beliefs. These processes are: the deductive fallacy, the inductive fallacy, and the cause-effect fallacy. Let me describe briefly how each of these fallacies works.

A *deductive fallacy* occurs when someone starts with a general belief and incorrectly concludes that, since this belief is true, other specific beliefs must be true. Sometimes the general premise is wrong, while at other times it is correct but the beliefs deduced from it are mistaken. A manager may, for example, believe that money is an incentive for employees and deduce from this that all employees are eager for more money, that a pay raise will lead to greater productivity, higher morale, and lower turnover, and that employees who receive a pay raise will express their appreciation by becoming more loyal to management. To begin with, it is questionable whether the initial premise is accurate. Even if it is, however, this manager is probably in for a disappointment when all these good things don't happen after the pay raise is given. This disappointment could be avoided if the manager were more fully aware of the complex relationship between productivity, morale, turnover, and incentives.

An *inductive fallacy* takes place when someone starts with one or more specific beliefs and incorrectly concludes that, since these beliefs are correct, a general premise must also be true. Again, the specific beliefs could be mistaken, and even if they are correct, the general conclusion for which they serve as evidence could be wrong. For example, Sara Clemens, new manager of the sales division, might believe that male employees are deliberately trying to keep contact with her as brief and formal as possible and that they are gossiping about her behind her back. From these specific beliefs she may draw the general conclusion that the male employees resent her because she got the management position. It is possible that Sara will simply accept this general conclusion without checking into the specific beliefs which led to the conclusion. If this happens, her beliefs may inhibit her ability to relate to the male employees in the division. If she seeks additional evidence to validate or invalidate the specific beliefs, she may find that not only the specific beliefs, but also the general conclusion is inaccurate or mistaken. Even if the initial beliefs are corroborated, she can use the additional evidence to help initiate a plan to deal with the problem.

The *cause-effect fallacy* occurs when someone mistakenly concludes that since two beliefs are true, one belief causes the other. One or both beliefs could be wrong, but even if they are correct, it could be incorrect to assume that one belief causes the other. To illustrate, during a staff meeting last week Tom Childs believed he was being more assertive than usual. Later during the same day he received a personnel evaluation which was lower than he believed he deserved. Tom concluded that his assertive behavior during the staff meeting caused the manager to give him a lower personnel evaluation. Since the manager completed the report before the staff meeting, Tom was mistaken. Unfortunately, Tom didn't try to find out if his belief was correct. Strongly convinced that he was right, he decided not to discuss the issue with the manager and filed a grievance with the union, instead. Needless to say, this mistaken conclusion caused unnecessary difficulty for Tom, the manager, the union, and other workers in the unit.

These believing processes, the deductive, inductive, and cause-effect fallacies, demonstrate people's tremendous capacity to "jump to conclusions." Of course, the ability to formulate conclusions is an importance characteristic of human beings. Conclusions can help people make decisions and exercise judgment in very complex situations. Nevertheless, conclusions are only as good as the specific facts and beliefs upon which they are based. People must strive to reach sound conclusions based upon the most solid evidence available, and be willing to consider new evidence in order to make effective decisions. On the other hand, jumping to conclusions based on mistaken beliefs and inadequate evidence will only decrease effectiveness. This latter process puts people in the position of spending most of their time struggling with their own illusive beliefs — like a boxer fighting his shadow.

In Part I, I explained that when people are confronted with new situations for the first time, they experience fear of varying intensity which motivates them to try to understand those situations. Once beliefs are established which help someone relate to a situation, the fear subsides. Usually fear plays a helpful role in the process of establishing beliefs. Once beliefs become established within personality, however, they resist change because they become a person's reality. When an established belief becomes threatened, fear reappears; only this time it protects the existing belief. This process can be positive or negative, depending upon the specific situation. If the belief is accurate and aids constructive behavior, then fear can mobilize the person to resist a change which might be a step backward. If the belief is mistaken and inhibits constructive behavior, however, fear can prevent the person from changing the belief and moving forward. Therefore, fear can be a blessing or a curse, depending upon the belief in question and the effect that belief has on one's life.

Our interest here is in how fear can prevent change in inhibiting beliefs. People vary tremendously in the degree to which they need their beliefs to be right. To understand these variations among people, we must look at the specific content of their beliefs. If you believe, for instance, that you need to be right all the time, you back yourself into a corner by your own belief, and set yourself up to become afraid when confronted with evidence that you're not right. Under these circumstances, your fear may even motivate you to become defensive and to deny the validity of any evidence that suggests your beliefs are wrong.

This situation would be very different if, instead of believing it was necessary for you to be right all the time, you believed it was all right to occasionally be wrong. This belief will give you more breathing room when confronted with evidence that you are wrong, and you will be less likely to become afraid and defend yourself. After considering the merits of the evidence, it is possible that you could use this new information to improve yourself.

People greatly restrict themselves whenever they conclude that their interpretation of something is the only one possible. Once a belief is fashioned this way, evidence to the contrary becomes especially threatening. Many people waste hours defending beliefs of this kind, when they could engage in more constructive activity. This is particularly wasteful when the beliefs are based on mistaken, inaccurate, or incomplete interpretations of experience. People would be better off if they regarded each of their beliefs as one from among a number of potential hypotheses available. This would allow them to more freely explore alternative hypotheses and change their beliefs if the evidence favors another interpretation. This type of perspective is an asset to those interested in learning as much as possible from their experiences.

It would be difficult to underestimate the impact that people's present beliefs (and fear generated by those beliefs) have on their ability to respond effectively in new situations. Let's take two employees with very different beliefs and show the effect that fear has on their decisions. Bob Davis believes that life is not something to be enjoyed but endured, that bad luck has prevented him from advancing in the company, and that other people are only interested in looking out for themselves. Since Bob always expects things to turn out wrong for him, he is afraid to try anything new. When he approaches a new situation or opportunity, he asks himself the question, "How can this hurt me?" Consequently, he is very defensive and unwilling to take the risks necessary to advance.

Nancy Bates, on the other hand, believes that life and work were meant to be enjoyed, that hard work rather than luck determines whether someone will advance in the company, and that other people basically have good intentions. Because Nancy expects things to work out all right as long as she does her best, she is not afraid to try new things. As she faces new situations, she asks herself, "How can I benefit from this opportunity?" This encourages her to be open to change and willing to take the risks necessary to advance.

There are people like Bob in every organization. In fact, I contend that most people in the work force become adjusted to levels of achievement which are less than their potential. The primary reason for this is that they have descriptive beliefs which underestimate their capabilities. They may not be aware that they could achieve more because current beliefs regarding their performance have been accepted as reality, and they are afraid to try anything new. In essence, they allow their own beliefs to literally scare them into immobility. In addition, the need for emotional security frequently motivates people to seek other people and environmental situations compatible with their view of reality. This makes it even more difficult for them to realize that their beliefs are keeping them from greater achievement. As a supervisor, one of the most important contributions you can make is to help employees rid themselves of inhibiting descriptive beliefs.

Evaluative Beliefs

While descriptive beliefs are interpretations regarding what is correct or incorrect, *evaluative beliefs* define what is good or bad. Perhaps comparing a descriptive belief with an evaluative belief will help clarify the distinction. Consider the statement, "Thorough knowledge of motivation is necessary for anyone to manage effectively." This descriptive belief asserts that a relationship exists between knowledge of motivation and a manager's effectiveness. By observing human behavior or conducting a scientific experiment, we could gather empirical data to determine how valid this statement is. If the evidence is negative or inconclusive, we can modify the belief to make it more accurate. Now consider the statement "Thorough knowledge of motivation is good for any manager." Can this be proven correct or incorrect? It is very difficult to validate or invalidate evaluative beliefs because, by definition, they are subjective conclusions dependent on one's criteria for "good" and "bad." Most people, of course, do not offer this level of definition when stating evaluative beliefs. In fact, they are usually only vaguely aware of their definitions for good and bad.

When someone states an opinion with which we disagree, we frequently aren't sure how to respond. Arguing frequently leads nowhere because it's our opinion against theirs. An expression we often hear is, "You're entitled to your opinion." The most common thing that happens when someone states an opinion we don't share is that we say nothing and simply listen. This behavior represents a tacit agreement that we will listen to other people's opinions, if they'll listen to ours. Although this provides an atmosphere within which we can feel safe to express our opinions, it undermines the type of give-and-take necessary to help people more fully examine the basis upon which opinions are held.

Although validating or invalidating evaluative beliefs is difficult, there are a few methods available to assist this process. To begin with, evaluative beliefs may be based on descriptive beliefs which are correct or incorrect. For example, the evaluative belief that thorough knowledge of motivation is good might stem from the descriptive belief that thorough knowledge of motivation is necessary to manage effectively.

People commonly fail to see how descriptive beliefs serve as the foundation for their evaluative beliefs. If someone presents an opinion that we don't help explore the premises behind, we may inadvertently reinforce an evaluative belief based on mistaken descriptive beliefs. Remember that when people tell you their opinions and you simply listen, they will be trying to read your nonverbal behavior to see if you agree or disagree with them. It is quite possible for your nonverbal behavior to convey that you agree with the opinion, while you strongly disagree. By reinforcing an evaluative belief which might stem from incorrect interpretations of experience, you could actually make it more difficult for the evaluative belief to be changed.

Another major way of scrutinizing evaluative beliefs is more subjective. It can be phrased, "Does the belief tend to promote or interfere with behavior which can help maximize one's potential?" I have maintained that beliefs guide action, and that actions will be different depending upon what the beliefs are and how they are used by people making daily decisions. People's evaluative beliefs greatly affect their choices. Some of these choices will help people move in a positive direction, while others will hold them back or cause them to go in a negative direction. My view is that evaluative beliefs which inhibit growth are excess baggage which ought to be discarded. What difference does it make if you can produce evidence to support an opinion, when the result of holding that opinion is that you become less effective. We need to assess the consequences of evaluative beliefs for ourselves and others. It would be helpful whenever you form an opinion about whether something is good or bad to also ask yourself, "What effect will this belief have on my life or on the lives of those with whom I come into contact?" If we routinely took stock of our evaluative beliefs, we would not only have a better basis for determining if the interpretations behind them are correct, but for deciding if the beliefs are worth having.

Let's use an example to underscore these points. Dave Roberts believes that it is bad to fail at anything. For years he systematically avoided any situation in which there was a possibility of failure. Thus, he passed up many opportunities for promotion. When thinking about his career, he realized that he wasn't going anywhere and was tired of seeing less qualified people get ahead while he stayed behind. It finally occurred to him that in order to advance, he had to attempt to succeed in activities where his skills were not well developed. His belief that failure was bad had to be discarded.

Dave began volunteering for new assignments. Some of his initial attempts lead to failure, but Dave found that he was able to learn things from those experiences which helped him the next time. From this, Dave developed a belief that opportunities to learn are good. This belief was instrumental in giving him the courage necessary to try things he previously avoided. Sustained by his new belief, Dave developed the skills and confidence which helped him successfully compete for promotions. Without this change in evaluative beliefs, Dave might never have taken the risks necessary for him to advance in his career.

Values

In Part I, I indicated that values are enduring beliefs in the desirability of engaging in certain processes (e.g., being honest, helpful) or striving to attain certain outcomes (e.g., self-respect, wisdom, wealth). Values guide our behavioral choices toward the fulfillment of those survival and growth needs we believe worth pursuing. Values develop during childhood and adolescence, and are usually well established into a value system by adulthood. Values are one's purposes — they define a person's meaning in life. Once established, there is a tendency for any value to resist change because it is linked with the satisfaction of needs. In fact, people's values become so much a part of their personalities that it is often difficult for them to imagine themselves with a different set of values.

Since values are subjective beliefs about what is worthwhile in life, they cannot be proven right or wrong. We can, however, look at them in terms of their behavioral consequences. One of the biggest misconceptions that people have about values is that they are entirely benevolent and positive aspects of personality. Unfortunately, values can lead to very destructive and negative results. The highest achievements of the human race have been motivated by values, but so have wars, discrimination, hate, crime, riots, and other malevolent human behavior.

Another common misconception is that it is taboo for anyone to question another person's values. All values are not equally effective in helping people live up to their potential. Values vary tremendously in how much they permit a person to grow and change. And even though you are limited to observing the consequences of behavior as the primary means of assessing the impact of values, you must strengthen your skills in this area if you hope to fully develop the human resources under your supervision.

To fully appreciate the many ways that values can interfere with change, it is useful to note that people can possess both *genuine* and *bogus* values. A *genuine value* is one that people actually believe desirable and use as a guide for behavior. In contrast, a *bogus value* is one that people do not really believe desirable but utilize to disguise the real (genuine) value motivating their behavior. Stated another way, *genuine values are values of conviction, while bogus values are values of convenience.* The two most common situations in which people employ bogus values are when they are trying to (1) protect their self-concept from something which is believed to be threatening or (2) surreptitiously manipulate the thinking or behavior of others to their own advantage.

Protecting the Self-Concept

I said that people are motivated to both improve themselves and maintain the integrity of their personalities. I also stressed that protecting personality takes precedence over other motives. The self-concept, of course, is a crucial component of personality. One of the most important purposes of values is to assist people in attempting to preserve and enhance their self-concepts. Any value can be used for this purpose.

In emphasizing the self-protective function of values, Rokeach indicates that "values provide a basis for rational self-justification insofar as possible, but also a basis for rationalized self-justification insofar as necessary" (1973, p. 13). Whenever a value is used as a rationalization, it is a bogus value. The problem is that people are frequently unaware that they are using their values as rationalizations. Although there are many situations when people might use bogus values to protect their self-concept, the two most common are fear of failure and fear of others' disapproval.

Many people believe that failure at something is a serious threat to their self-concept. When faced with the possibility of failure they experience fear often so severe that they are driven to reduce it. People who are faced with a fear of failure have many options, but two common ones are to avoid or escape the fear-producing situation. Under these circumstances, bogus values can be very useful. Such values can allow people to look good to themselves and others, while reducing fear. In other words, they permit a person to appear noble on the basis of stated convictions or to champion one cause as a way of covering up their fear of another. Unfortunately, bogus values always seem reasonable on the surface, which is precisely why they make such convincing rationalizations. People can even fool themselves with bogus values. They may be totally unaware that they are stressing a certain value to protect themselves from a situation they fear, and that the value would probably have little or no meaning to them if it weren't for that fear.

I'll use an illustration to highlight these dynamics. Sally Karpinsky graduated from college believing that she could only be effective teaching. Since the number of teaching positions available that year was rather limited, she ended up interviewing for a variety of jobs. At the end of one job interview, she was offered a position in management with a major firm. She was so convinced that she couldn't handle the job, however, that she decided not to try. She turned down the offer and made a quick decision to attend graduate school instead. That evening she told her parents that after giving the matter a great deal of thought, she had decided that furthering her education was the most important thing to her then. This decision sounded so logical that no one questioned her real motives. The fact that she had placed a bogus value on further education to escape the possibility of failure in the management position went unrecognized, even by Sally herself.

The problem with bogus values like this is that they keep a person from overcoming their fears. For someone to achieve full potential in life, it is almost always necessary to take chances. If people develop values which keep them from taking those chances, they may be cheating themselves out of real opportunities. Something else which frequently happens is that the beliefs behind bogus values are mistaken or inaccurate. For example, Sally may be perfectly capable of handling the management position offered to her. She is convinced, however, that she can't handle it, even though she has no experience upon which to base this belief. At least, her belief is incomplete. Unfortunately, she won't be able to find out for sure since she turned the job down out of fear.

People can also use bogus values to justify their actions when they fear-disapproval from others. One of the most intriguing characteristics of people is their ability to maintain self-regard in spite of the consequences of their actions. Even when their actions have negative results, people can convince both themselves and others that they are right. Let me highlight this process with an example. Sam Barnes is a manager in a manufacturing company. One day he noticed that several unskilled laborers were joking quite a bit on the job. Sam gave them a warning and indicated that he expected absolute obedience, but their joking persisted. So, he decided to teach them all a lesson by randomly selecting one employee to fire for insubordination. Most employees regarded this act as a severe reaction to the problem and very unfair; therefore, a delegation of employees met with the owner to express their views. When the owner talked to Sam, he justified his action by saying that the cooperation of employees was essential for the company to meet its production goals. This explanation sounded so convincing to the owner that the decision was allowed to stand. Stating a bogus value for cooperation allowed Sam to avoid the owner's disapproval.

The major problem with bogus values used to protect the self-concept is that they provide a means for people to avoid something they fear which at the same time prevents them from pursuing genuine values. In Part IV, I will discuss how modifying mistaken beliefs can help someone give up bogus values of this kind. I contend that we should do this whenever feasible to prevent people from wasting time and energy defending themselves against their own inaccurate beliefs.

Manipulating Others

Bogus values are also used to secretly manipulate the thinking or behavior of others. This type of bogus value functions much like a "hidden agenda"; a person states or implies that his or her intention is one thing when it is actually something else. For example, a highly ambitious employee tells a colleague that she values her friendship, when her real intention is to gain this colleague's confidence and perhaps some information that can be used to accelerate her career climb—the real value. Frequently, it is possible to see through bogus values used in this way and to identify the real value being pursued. The primary clue is a discrepancy between what people say they value and their subsequent behavior. It is crucial for managers to develop ability to spot such discrepancies, since this kind of bogus value is frequently used by people to resist change.

Lack of Values

In addition to bogus values, there are many other ways that values, or the lack of them, cause resistance. For example, occasionally people have the talent to excel in a certain area, but they simply do not hold values which would motivate them to develop that talent. In situations like this, we could not expect them to begin developing that talent until they have established new values.

At other times, people have values which would permit them to develop their potential, but these values are not dominant enough in their value system to significantly influence the choices they make. For example, Jack Thomas places a high value on family security but a relatively low value on achievement. As a manager in an electronics firm, he earns a good salary and provides well for his family. There is not much likelihood, however, that Jack will be able to move any higher in his company unless he moves to one of its other plants in another city. Jack has had several offers, but his family is reluctant to move. Since Jack values family security more than achievement, he will probably turn down the offers and remain where he is.

Both family security and achievement are noble values. As I said earlier, all values sound good on the surface. It is only when we look at their behavioral consequences that we can compare them. In Jack's case, staying where he is might be the best choice; however, it would be hard to know for certain unless we thoroughly examined his situation at home and at work. One thing is clear: his preference for family security over achievement leads to a different result than if the relative importance attached to these values was reversed. Frequently, helping people increase the dominance (intensity) of certain values in their value system is the most effective way to promote positive change.

Finally, people sometimes pursue dominant values related to areas of potential talent but behave ineffectively. Frequently this is caused by a skill deficiency which could be corrected by appropriate training. In this case, people aren't resisting change — they simply don't know how to change. Since they already have values which would motivate them to develop their talent, it is likely that they will be receptive to an opportunity for training.

PART III

Finding the Causes of Resistance

Principles in Assessing **7** *Resistance*

Your Resistance Is Showing

Let me begin this chapter with a bold statement: You have no business trying to overcome resistance in someone else, or even complaining about it, if you yourself are unwilling to change. As a manager, you should be a role model that your employees can emulate when faced with a situation in which change would be constructive. Before you can function effectively as such a role model, you need to ask yourself some difficult but challenging questions, and to be honest enough to admit it when your answers are less than completely favorable:

- Do you have facts, beliefs, or values which inhibit your ability to change? If so, what are they?

- Have you examined the implications of your facts, beliefs, and values for yourself and others?

- Which of your beliefs might be based on mistaken interpretations of your experience?

- What evidence do you have to substantiate your facts and beliefs?

- Are you willing to scrutinize your facts, beliefs, and values regularly to see what part they play in either promoting or interfering with your willingness to change?

- If you recognize a value or belief which restricts positive change, are you willing to change it?

- If someone confronts you with evidence contrary to your facts or beliefs, do you have the courage to consider that evidence without becoming defensive?

Obviously, none of us can claim a "perfect score" in response to these questions. To do so would deny our humanity. Some people go through life quite comfortably without systematically dealing with the above questions. You, on the other hand, cannot afford this luxury. As someone who makes daily decisions which have a direct impact on others, you have a responsibility to make sure that those decisions are the best ones possible. You cannot adequately do this unless you are thoroughly aware of the facts, beliefs, and values which enter into those decisions. What's more, no one can force you to do this; it has to be something you do voluntarily. My goal is to convince you that scrutinizing your facts, values, and beliefs is prerequisite to effective management, so that you will want to do this.

There are several reasons why your willingness to recognize factors which interfere with your ability to develop and change are particularly important. To begin with, as a manager your actions are visible to both your superiors and those under your immediate supervision. You will be expected to be a "clear thinker" capable of logically evaluating a situation by considering all relevant variables, then arriving at the most rational conclusion. Much of your credibility hinges on how adequately you do this. Managers who do not think logically are labeled "irrational," "impulsive," "stubborn," "bullheaded," and "egotistical." Needless to say, if people believe you are what any of these words imply, it will have a negative impact on how they relate to you.

If you do not consider all relevant factors, including your own beliefs and vested interests, chances are your decisions won't be as good as they could be. If others view you as someone not open to alternative views, they might not bother to share ideas with you. This will prevent you from receiving information you need to make the best possible decisions. By remaining open to others' ideas and being willing to modify your own views, you will be creating a climate conducive to positive change.

Another factor you need to keep in mind is the possibility that your actions could actually be the source of resistance among others. If you stubbornly hold onto your own beliefs and insist that your way is right in spite of others' opinions, you increase the likelihood that your way will be openly or subtly resisted. There are times, of course, when you will need to make decisions that your employees don't like, and it is quite possible that you can never make a decision that everyone will agree with. This is one of the hard facts about being a manager. Nevertheless, if your employees see you as being open to their views, and willing to objectively hear them out when a difference of opinion exists, they will be more likely to support you even if your decision is not what they want.

It is crucial that your employees regard you as being fair; it is devastating to be seen as arbitrary, capricious, or insensitive to the needs and wishes of others. And remember, your employees are capable of believing that you are all these bad things, even if you're not. To reduce the possibility that others will develop mistaken beliefs about you, it is necessary to supply them with regular evidence that you are both unbiased and open to the ideas of others.

A final consideration, perhaps the most crucial, is that the actions you take based on your beliefs and values affect people — for better or worse. Accordingly, you always have to guard against the possibility that your beliefs about employees are mistaken or that your values are interfering with their development. For example, if you believe that Joe Cardwell is incapable of learning enough to succeed at more demanding jobs, you may decide consciously or unconsciously that you shouldn't waste time helping Joe improve. It could be, however, that Joe is capable of learning, but you are unable to teach him what he needs to know. Your belief provides you with an excuse not to spend much time with Joe, while it deprives him of the opportunity to advance within the company. Just because you've tried everything you know to help someone like Joe doesn't mean that you've exhausted alternatives. There may be methods you're not aware of, or you might not be the best one to work with Joe. Here it would be imperative to examine your beliefs and the actions which result from them. If you resist doing this and insist that you're right, you may deprive someone of a chance to become a more effective and capable employee.

Identifying Resistance in Others

Any fact, belief, or value held by an individual or shared by a group can be used to resist change. Accordingly, I am now going to turn attention to helping you increase the extent to which you can identify the many ways these variables cause resistance in others. Since the facts, beliefs, and values held by others are mental constructs which we can't literally "see," the role they play in creating resistance is difficult to isolate. Difficult but not impossible. The process of accurately identifying these variables will never be reduced to an exact science which allows us to tell with certainty what is behind a given case of resistance. Instead, we must try to do the best we can, in spite of limitations.

Fortunately, we have a powerful source of information to help us with our task — observation of what people say and do. Values, beliefs, and facts can be inferred in this manner. In fact, this is the only way we can identify a person's values, beliefs, and facts. Everything someone says or does is a clue which can provide insight into the ways that these variables cause resistance. This source of information has been there all along, it just hasn't been fully utilized. Consequently, attempts to deal with resistance are often unsystematic and inadequate.

It is very risky to try to assess the causes of resistance by observing only what a person does. Watching people in action supplies clues, but additional information from what they say is almost always necessary to accurately pinpoint the source, focus, and intensity of resistance. For example, consider the following things employees might do which could indicate resistance:

- Come late to work

- Return late from lunch or coffee breaks

- Abuse sick leave benefits

- Come late to meetings

- Rush through meetings

- Fail to implement changes agreed to at a meeting

- Refuse to cooperate with others

- Avoid or ignore others

- Remain silent when discussion would be appropriate

- Spend a lot of job time discussing personal matters

- Make unnecessary mistakes

- Neglect work assignments

- Take too much time to complete assignments

- Spend much time on unimportant assignments and not enough on important ones

- Incorrectly implement new policies or procedures

- Refuse to implement new policies or procedures

- Accept inferior quality performance from employees

- Avoid opportunities for advancement

- Make little effort to improve work-related knowledge and skills

- File personnel grievances

- Request a transfer to another department

- Frequently apply for job openings elsewhere

By simply observing employees doing these things, we can't conclude that they are signs of resistance. Also, even if resistance is involved, more information is needed before we can draw any firm inferences regarding the source, focus, and intensity of resistance. Without a clear picture of the causes of resistance, our efforts to reduce it are likely to be misguided. Let me demonstrate some pitfalls of forming premature conclusions from what a person does. I will talk about this in reference to beliefs, then show how it can happen with values.

The Difficulty of Inferring Beliefs from What Someone Does

I recommend that you observe both what people say and do in trying to discover what they really believe. The reasons for this are:

1. Any specific act could represent multiple possible beliefs.
2. People can act the same even though the beliefs behind their behavior are very different.
3. People can base their acts on mistaken beliefs not readily apparent to you or them.

In addition, people are capable of doing things inconsistent with their beliefs. Some people, for example, might sign a petition asking for higher wages not because they believe they deserve more money, but because of peer pressure. If you saw these people signing the petition and assumed it was because they believed they were underpaid, you would be making an error. In this case, you could learn much more by talking to the people than by only observing what they do. This would also help you avoid forming false conclusions.

The key thing to determine about beliefs is whether or not they are based on accurate or inaccurate interpretations of experience. Of course, resistance can and frequently does stem from beliefs based on solid empirical evidence. Resistance of this kind is usually much more difficult to eliminate than resistance which can be traced to mistaken or inaccurate interpretations of experience, because people are resisting with "good reason." It may be necessary to change your change. As a manager you can expect to encounter resistance which emerges from the full range of beliefs, extending from the most rational to the most irrational. Therefore, it is imperative that you are aware of the basis upon which beliefs are held, so that you can effectively deal with resistance when it develops.

The Difficulty of Inferring Values from What Someone Does

In Part I we noted that everything someone does reflects values because values represent convictions about desirable pursuits. This doesn't necessarily mean that the value is obvious, however. Sometimes people engage in unvalued activity, in order to pursue something which is valued. For example, a man may be cleaning up trash at the end of a work day, even though this is not a job requirement. On the surface it may appear that he values cleanliness. If we examine the reasons for this behavior, we may find that he greatly dislikes cleaning but does it because he believes it will help him keep his job. In this instance, job security and not cleanliness is the value motivating his behavior. To discover the full meaning of his actions we wouldn't get far by merely observing what he does. Talking to him could reveal the purpose of his behavior, and give us evidence about his beliefs and values which would otherwise remain hidden.

We can also tell a lot about people's values by observing what they don't do. When people choose not to do something, this is evidence that they may lack certain values. Before reaching any conclusion about this, however, other factors must be ruled out. I have previously discussed the inhibiting role which fear plays in causing people to espouse bogus values. A person may want to do something but decide not to, because of fear. Bogus values can be used to help someone avoid or escape what is feared. At other times, people select an action, not because that particular activity serves a value, but because they are afraid not to. In many of these situations, security is the value motivating behavior, although it may appear that some other value guides them. People have both survival and growth needs, and situational factors will always affect decisions about the values a person will act on. When fear is intense, security values tend to push other values into the background.

I want to remind you that people's beliefs often play a prominent, if disguised, role in these processes. A belief may cause the fear, leading a person to pursue security as a value. Thus, additional data revealing the actual purposes served by someone's actions can be crucial.

Don't Jump to Conclusions

In your efforts to locate the causes of resistance, base your inferences on evidence you can clearly substantiate. You are on more solid ground if you say to yourself something like, "Her statement tells me that she believes my methods of management are ineffective," without giving in to the temptation to add, "therefore she must have something against me." As a general rule, never draw conclusions or make generalizations that go beyond what you can see and hear. Even here it is to your advantage to collect as much evidence as possible before inferring the cause of resistance and deciding on action.

Most importantly, keep an open mind which will allow you to consider additional evidence, especially if it contradicts previous inferences. You can't afford to develop a vested interest in your own conclusions. An unwillingness to objectively consider additional evidence is a sign of resistance on *your* part, which will get in the way of your ability to solve a problem. Stay humble. Don't tell yourself you need to be right; dealing with resistance is hard enough without having to fight yourself.

Build an Inventory of Facts, Beliefs, and Values Held by Others

Identifying facts, beliefs, and values held by others is an ongoing process, not a single event that occurs when resistance is encountered. As you work with employees over an extended period of time, you will have many opportunities to observe them in a wide variety of circumstances. You will be able to see what they say and do under routine conditions and during periods of change. Through this process, you can develop an inventory of facts, beliefs, and values held by each employee. If you invest the time and effort to do this, it will really pay off when you plan a change which will affect them. Your inventory will help you anticipate resistance and take steps to prevent it or keep it at a minimum.

In addition, the information in your inventory can be an invaluable resource whenever resistance surfaces. Without the inventory, you may be unable to understand why employees are saying or doing something to resist change. With the inventory, you can take a specific fact, belief, or value used to resist change and put it into perspective by relating it to other facts, beliefs, and values held by them. This will not only decrease your errors in identifying the causes of resistance, but also help you formlate more effective strategies for dealing with it.

Locating Specific Causes of **8** *Resistance*

Your ability to locate the cause of resistance in any particular case can be greatly enhanced if you ask yourself when listening, "What fact, belief, or value is being conveyed by what this person is saying?" Similarly, when observing what someone does, you can ask yourself, "What fact, belief, or value is being represented by what this person is doing?" By consistently asking yourself these questions, and putting the data together, not only will you come to understand your employees more fully, but you will be able to more effectively locate the causes of resistance when it occurs.

Now let's look at some specific things people say that can help you identify whether resistance is stemming from facts, descriptive beliefs, evaluative beliefs, or values. This information can be added to observations of what people do to help you understand why they are resisting change. The more accurate your assessment, the more likely that you will be able to prepare your employees for change — to take the path of least resistance.

FACTS

Again, when facts are used to resist change, the first thing you need to do is determine if they are actually *facts* (based on definitive evidence) and not *beliefs* (based on subjective interpretations). People often fail to make these distinctions in their mind and in the way they talk. Thus, people confuse facts with beliefs when they say "I know ...," "I'm convinced that ...," or "I'm absolutely sure that ...," when it is correct for them to say "It is my belief that ...." Watch carefully for beliefs presented as facts. If a statement can't be backed by definitive evidence, then it is a belief. It is especially important for you to make these distinctions because many people want their beliefs to sound like facts, in order to be more convincing.

Even when you have established that facts are being used, remember that facts can be and often are used selectively by people. Sometimes this is deliberate, while at other times it is unintentional. In either case, you must listen closely to people when they present facts and identify other relevant facts not brought into the open. Otherwise, your ability to see how the selective use of facts is fostering resistance will be greatly limited.

It is quite common to hear people state facts to resist change. For example, facts about failures are often advanced as reasons for not wanting to do something now or in the future. People can't know for a fact what is going to happen to them either one minute from now or at any future time. Nevertheless, people are quite capable of convincing themselves (and sometimes others) that they cannot succeed at something previously associated with failure. Helping employees put facts in perspective or become aware of additional facts relevant to an issue can help lower resistance to change. This is not only true for facts regarding previous failure but also for any other facts that cause resistance to change.

On some occasions it may be difficult to understand why a fact is mentioned at all. In these situations, your best bet is to look at the fact within the context of what's being discussed. If someone is trying to influence you, they will probably pick the most opportune time to state a revealing fact: that is, they will select the time within the discussion when presenting the fact will most benefit their case. Although you may detect the possibility that the fact is being used to resist change, it is wise to check the accuracy of your inference by gathering further information. Once someone states a fact, they are, in essence, showing their hand. You can follow up by asking, "Based on that fact, what do you think should be done?" This will allow you to avoid making an incorrect assumption about *why* the fact is being presented.

For example, facts about the work environment are often presented at just the right time to undermine a proposed change you are trying to implement. In other words, they are not brought out for added perspective, but to persuade you not to make the change you have in mind. Also, some facts about the work environment may be selectively presented while others are either ignored or minimized. If people disagree with your proposed change, frequently they develop their case against the change before discussing it with you; therefore, your ability to anticipate these arguments in advance will be crucial to lowering resistance. When it comes to facts about a situation, there is no substitute for accurate and thorough information — your best ally when others use facts to resist change. The worst position you can be in is caught off guard by someone else's facts. If you have to respond to someone's evidence off the top of your head, you will be less able to handle this in the most effective manner. Do your homework! Following are a few typical statements of "fact" which are commonly used to resist change. Please feel free to use your own experience to add to this list.

Facts about self

- My doctor told me I shouldn't subject myself to too much stress.
- All my friends are in this department.
- I've been in this job thirty years.
- I never had a course in accounting.
- I've never written a proposal before.
- I failed math in high school.
- On an aptitude test I came out really low in that area.

Facts about others

- They went bankrupt in their last deal.
- He's on probation in his present job.
- Joe's college grades weren't that good. Why should we give him the promotion?
- I understand she has three children.
- Other companies that buy supplies from them say they rarely deliver on time.
- He's black, you know.
- I hope you're aware that she's a leader in the local women's movement.
- Their profit-loss statement has never been good.

Facts about the work environment

- The company pays less than any other electronics firm in town.
- Remember that the turnover rate is already 25% higher this year.
- I hope you realize that personnel grievances have been increasing during the past six months.
- Our office already has more people in it than any other office. How can you expect us to work effectively if you move more employees in here?
- We haven't been given any training.
- Why should we do that? We haven't received an increase in fringe benefits in four years.

DESCRIPTIVE BELIEFS

The relationship between facts and beliefs is very complex. Sometimes facts are the major cause of resistance, and if they can be identified and placed in perspective, associated beliefs may also change. At other times, beliefs are the major cause of resistance, and identifying and dealing with seemingly relevant facts will have no effect upon the beliefs. Perhaps the main reason for this is that beliefs are more difficult to prove or disprove. It is not uncommon for people to hold onto beliefs, even though you can produce substantial evidence against them. Of course, when you first spot signs of resistance, it is usually difficult to tell if the primary cause is facts, beliefs, or a combination. Only when you begin to piece together many bits of information will the relationship between these variables become clear.

Recall that *descriptive beliefs* are subjective interpretations of what is correct and incorrect. We formulate descriptive beliefs to help us understand past and present, and to predict what will happen. In short, descriptive beliefs allow us to make sense out of experiences so that we have a basis on which to make decisions.

Sometimes people develop beliefs that they will be unsuccessful at something even though they have had no previous experience with it. I have a difficult time understanding the pervasive fear of failure in our society. Perhaps it is the tremendous premium we place on success. But how can anyone succeed at anything unless they place themselves under conditions where the possibility of failure exists? Avoiding situations in which people could gain competence has got to be one of the main reasons for incompetence. The resulting waste of potential talent in our work force is staggering.

It's almost as if people are saying something like, "I would if I could, but I can't, so I won't try." Although I've heard this often, it continues to surprise me. It is a good example of people's inability to accurately evaluate the content of their own beliefs, and the implications those beliefs have on their choices. Essentially, people who say this indicate that they elect to believe that they will fail at something even before they try. In many instances, it is simply inaccurate for them to say, "I can't," unless they have a handicap or genuinely lack the capability or desire to perform the task. When this type of statement is used, it is often supported by underlying negative descriptive beliefs. To help employees feel comfortable trying the feared activity, you would first need to identify the beliefs involved. Often they have little to do with the situation at hand. Taking steps to change such beliefs and getting people to do what they previously believed impossible is one of the most important challenges and rewards of being in management.

Another common situation is when the initial efforts of people to do something are less than successful and they develop a belief that they will be unable to succeed at this in the future. This belief is represented in such statements as, "I've never been very good at that, and I don't think I ever will be," or "I tried that once and it didn't work out; I don't see any point in trying again." The most damaging thing about statements like these is that a belief regarding past performance is used to conclude that future efforts will also fail. But how can someone know what will happen in the future? Will the conditions in the future be the same as those in the past? The words "I will fail" make this sound preordained and that there's no way to change it. Although stated as a fact, this is actually a belief. Therefore, when you hear employees making statements like these to resist doing something, you should help them examine their evidence. Also it is often helpful to assist them in envisioning more positive outcomes — to see themselves *doing it.* With some successful experiences, the "I will fail" part often disappears, and new opportunities may open for the person.

Also be aware that people don't like to admit that they are afraid of failure, or that they have negative beliefs about their abilities. They especially don't want to admit this to their supervisor. In fact, sometimes they don't even want to admit it to themselves. If you observe them closely enough, however, such beliefs will usually show up in what they say or do. For example, if people seem to avoid situations, if they don't make any suggestions during staff meetings when this would be appropriate, inhibiting descriptive beliefs may be involved.

When you initiate something new, a wide range of descriptive beliefs can be used to resist the change. For example, descriptive beliefs about others are often used for this purpose. These beliefs frequently take the form of critical descriptions of others' weaknesses or limitations. Examples are "He could never learn to do this job," and "She would have a difficult time getting used to our tight production schedules." When beliefs like these are stated, probe for information which will allow you to accurately pinpoint the reason for the resistance. Asking such questions as "Could you tell me more about why you feel the way you do?" can help you do this.

In addition, negative descriptive beliefs about the work environment are frequently responsible for resistance to change. These beliefs are reflected in statements like, "This company doesn't care about its employees," and "It's impossible to get ahead around here." Since they can easily lead to anger, frustration, and other contagious emotions, it is important that you structure situations where these beliefs can be aired objectively. There is no substitute for being viewed as a manager willing to listen and to give opinions an impartial hearing. If employees don't come to you to discuss their beliefs about a situation, it will be difficult for you to identify all relevant factors causing resistance. Of course, being regarded as a manager who is fair develops over time. Your actions are visible and you will need to prove yourself to employees. If you don't make a conscious effort to do this, it may turn out that you are the major cause of resistance in your organization. Following is another list of typical statements designed to aid you in locating descriptive beliefs that may be causing resistance.

Descriptive beliefs about self

- I wouldn't be able to do that.
- I don't think I could accept that change.
- I'm too busy to do this.
- I couldn't handle moving to another department.
- I'm too shy to work in a large group.
- I don't have the energy for that much responsibility.

- I'm a follower, not a leader.
- I don't think I'll ever learn these new procedures.

Descriptive beliefs about others

- I don't think moving her to another department would solve the problem.
- I wouldn't discuss this with him because he can't keep anything to himself.
- He pretends to be busy to avoid additional work.
- He makes these changes just to harass us.
- If you tell her, she might hold it against you.
- She never seems to understand our point of view.
- He always passes the buck to someone else.
- People around here seem to be more concerned with protecting their security than anything else.

Descriptive beliefs about the work environment

- We're underpaid for what we're asked to do.
- The fringe benefits offered by this company are really low.
- In this company, it's not what you know, it's who you know that counts.
- We're evaluated too frequently.
- This organization would never accept that idea.
- Opportunities for promotion around here only go to those who don't make waves.

EVALUATIVE BELIEFS

Evaluative beliefs are subjective interpretations regarding what is good or bad. Like descriptive beliefs, evaluative beliefs both help us understand the past and present, and decide what to do in the future. The difference is that while descriptive beliefs allow us to describe or explain something, evaluative beliefs are used to form judgments. It is well known how judgmental people can be. Of course, the capacity to form judgments may be a blessing or curse depending upon how they are used. If you are proposing a change that employees believe is "good," chances are they will support it. If they believe the proposed change is "bad," however, the probability is increased that they will resist it. Hence, you need to be concerned with people's definitions for "good" and "bad" as they apply to specific situations.

Evaluative beliefs also concern the "worth" people assign to themselves, others, and the work environment. Whether people like themselves and the quality of their work are key factors in determining if they will resist change. Consider the statements "I guess my low score on that test proves again how stupid I am," and "I knew I would fail (which means I'm incompetent)." It is rare for people to actually say these things to someone else, but it is quite common for them to form private negative judgments about themselves. Let's examine these two statements.

In the first statement a fact (low test score) is used as evidence that the person is stupid. People who have such evaluative beliefs about themselves can usually produce an abundance of factual evidence to substantiate their beliefs. Unfortunately, they often fail to consider that anyone who tries to do something new is bound to have setbacks, and that people can learn from those setbacks. In the second statement, a descriptive belief stated as a fact is given as evidence that the person is inadequate. The statement can't qualify as a fact because the person could not know in advance that he would fail.

Whether based on facts or descriptive beliefs, negative evaluative beliefs of this kind will almost always inhibit the willingness of people to work up to their potential. People who have such beliefs tend to be depressed, apathetic, and passive. As a result, they usually defer to the judgment of others or avoid any situation where they may be asked to take initiative; good clues that they have such beliefs about themselves. Since they have condemned themselves with their own beliefs, they are seldom willing to take risks. Needless to say, such people need no enemies, and you can anticipate that they will resist changes you seek. Their negativism prevents them from looking forward to anything new. People who have such low regard for themselves are hard to work with, because they screen everything through a negative self-concept. Before their readiness to change can be increased, you will probably need to do something about their inhibiting evaluative beliefs. Perhaps the single most effective thing you can do is to take care in placing such employees in situations where they will be successful. A few victories can go a long way toward helping people get rid of negative evaluative beliefs about themselves.

It is also possible for people to use evaluative beliefs about others as a way of resisting change. There are two major ways that this usually happens. The first way is to speak highly of other people so they will get stuck with an assignment. In situations like this, your task will be to identify if people genuinely believe someone else would be better for a certain task, if they are trying to pass the buck, or if they are afraid of the task for some reason. Observing what people do and say over time will provide you with clues that you can use to determine if praise for others is being used as a form of resistance. People are often duped into doing things which others don't want to do, because they are so flattered by the praise that they don't see the real motivation.

The second way is to speak very negatively about others. One of the things which puzzles me is how quickly people label others as incompetent. People rarely state this openly to another person; such remarks are usually reserved for informal conversations between two or more people discussing someone else who isn't present. Through this process, beliefs about the competence of others are established then spread through the grapevine. The basis of these beliefs is seldom scrutinized, and the person who is the brunt of the beliefs is unable to present the other side. This is unfortunate and potentially damaging because such beliefs are bound to inhibit the relationship between those who hold the belief and the person regarded as being incompetent. This person is pronounced guilty before the defense can present its case.

Perhaps even more puzzling is that people who label others as incompetent, almost always see themselves as competent. In addition, it seldom occurs to them that others might regard them as incompetent. It is indeed an interesting piece of mental gymnastics for people to believe that others are incompetent while also believing that they, by contrast, are not only worthy of high esteem but deserve to be regarded as competent. My own opinion is that deep inside people are afraid that they might not be competent, and one way they can verify this is by comparing themselves to others. Since people need to come out on top in such comparisons, they quickly see their own strengths and more quickly see others' weaknesses. The best way for people to insure a favorable balance between beliefs about their competence and others' incompetence is to keep all this to themselves — except for occasional, discreet references about the inadequacy of others.

Of course, people can develop negative evaluative beliefs about others which relate to issues besides competence. Sometimes they stem from lack of respect which develops from previous experience or misunderstanding. At other times they may come from prejudicial attitudes ("Blacks are no good") or from envy, jealousy, or competitiveness. Then there are times when people simply don't like each other for reasons that they can't adequately define ("There's just something about him").

Frequently when differences between people are identified and resolved, the negative evaluative beliefs dissolve; at other times, however, people stubbornly maintain their beliefs even though there is no real justification for them. As a manager you should do whatever you can to bring the reasons for such beliefs to the surface. You may not be able to get people to like each other, but you can insist that they don't allow personal feelings to interfere with their ability to meet job requirements.

In your efforts to bring about change, you may also encounter resistance from negative evaluative beliefs about the work environment. You need to identify the conditions causing these beliefs, because they frequently lead to lower rates of production, higher turnover, and a greater incidence of grievances. Also determine if evaluative beliefs regarding working conditions are the actual cause of resistance. Sometimes negative statements about working conditions are used as a convenient scapegoat for beliefs about oneself or others. Gathering additional evidence will help you uncover the actual beliefs and the reasons for them.

Again, here's a list of typical statements. Heard any of these?

Evaluative beliefs about self

- I'm not very good at dealing with other people.
- You can give me that assignment, but I know I'll do a bad job.
- I'm terrible at putting my thoughts in writing.
- I'm about as inept at this as anybody could be.
- Let's face it, I'm just a failure.

- I'm much better at other things than this.
- Nobody listens to me. (I must be a fool.)

Evaluative beliefs about others

- He's very qualified, let's give him this project.
- I think we can all agree that Steve has the personality necessary to handle such a delicate matter.
- Mary, I got tied up on some other assignments. Could you handle this for me? You're better at this sort of thing than I am anyway.
- There's just something about her I don't like.
- He's the worst employee I've ever worked with.
- I don't think he's sharp enough to do this work.
- She's so self-centered. I bet she never takes our feelings into consideration.
- He's friendly enough, but . . .

Evaluative beliefs about the work environment

- This is a lousy place to work.
- This job stinks.
- We have the worst management structure I've ever seen.
- The pay and fringe benefits here are terrible.
- The training offered by this company is a complete waste of time.
- It was the best job I could find at the time . . .

VALUES

Once again, values are a person's beliefs about what is worth pursuing in life. I'd like to remind you of the distinction between genuine and bogus values, which I made in chapter 6. A *genuine value* is one that people truly believe worthy of pursuit and use as a guide for behavior. By way of contrast, a *bogus value* is one that people do not really believe desirable but use to disguise the true (genuine) value behind their behavior. It is inconsistent to say people have a genuine value unless they choose behavior that serves that value, unless they truly attempt to attain it.

You should realize that both genuine and bogus values can cause resistance to change, although they do so in different ways. In the case of genuine values, resistance frequently stems from a conflict between what people value and what you want them to do. When this is true, you may have to change plans. At other times, people may simply not have a genuine value that relates to what you want them to do. If so, you can often help them develop one. Bogus values, on the other hand, are stated as a way of disguising the real cause of the resistance. You will have to gather additional evidence to discover why the bogus value is being used, so that the actual cause of resistance can be identified.

To highlight these distinctions, let's use a value for politeness as an example. Some people may genuinely value politeness because they believe that being polite is a constructive way of developing relationships with others. In contrast, other people may hold a bogus value for politeness because they believe others will disapprove of them if they are not polite, and further believe that such disapproval is bad and should be avoided. In this instance, politeness is a bogus value because instead of being pursued for its own sake, the purpose served by it is to avoid others' disapproval.

You don't have to become expert in spotting bogus values. My primary goal is to make you aware that bogus values exist and that they, along with genuine values, can cause resistance to change. Perhaps the most important thing is to become an expert at spotting genuine value conflicts. These can be very powerful and should usually be treated as a reason for negotiation and replanning. Some common statements that reflect values are given below.

Values pertaining to self

- I know you want me to apply for that promotion, but I prefer the job I have now.
- I don't place a high priority on attending training programs.
- It's not important to me to have more authority.
- I don't want to change. I'm perfectly content to stay the way I am now.
- Some people enjoy power and prestige, but I see these as meaningless goals for myself.
- That may be important to you, but it's not to me.
- I like working with my hands.

Values pertaining to others

- Let someone else help her; I'm just not interested.
- What you think really doesn't matter to me.
- Working with them is something I'd rather not do.
- There's no purpose in trying to cooperate with management.

- I don't see any reason to be honest with them.
- I'll never forgive him for doing that to me.
- You can do whatever you like.
- Frankly, my dear, I don't give a . . .

Values pertaining to the work environment

- Who cares what the goals are, I just do my job.
- I put a low priority on this type of work.
- The salary scale is less important to me than the fringe benefits.
- This job gives me a chance to work outdoors.
- I wouldn't be caught dead here, except . . .
- I'm just counting the days . . .

The Phenomenon of Complex Causes 9

In chapter 8, I provided guidelines for identifying specific facts, beliefs, and values which may be causing resistance. Although it is possible for resistance to stem from a single fact, belief, or value, this is exceptional. In addition, there is also the danger of identifying a symptom rather than the cause of resistance. Therefore, when you are trying to initiate change and someone makes a statement, you can't simply accept that statement at face value, because it may not be the cause of resistance. The cause may well be related facts, beliefs, and values someone holds that are not explicitly stated. In separating symptoms from causes your inventory of employee facts, beliefs, and values can be especially useful. The inventory will permit you to consider a specific statement in conjunction with other things you have observed the employee say and do previously. This will provide you more complete understanding of what's taking place at any particular time.

Of course, it's impossible to become aware of all of someone's facts, beliefs, and values, and it isn't necessary to do this when encountering resistance. In any situation certain of these variables will be more relevant than others as causes of resistance. These variables form what I define as a cluster. Therefore, as you attempt to put a specific statement into perspective, you need to identify any other related facts, beliefs, and values in that cluster. The inventory can be a resource here. It is crucial that you do this, otherwise your assessment will be based on incomplete information, and the problem may continue despite attempts at solutions.

To demonstrate how a statement can be related to a cluster of other facts, beliefs, and values, consider the statement, "Management by objectives is worthless." This is an evaluative belief explicitly stated. However, it could be tied directly to unstated facts, beliefs, and values, such as: "They tried that in X corporation and concluded that it was a total failure" (fact), "I'm not interested in implementing it here" (value), "I don't think I could measure up under a more demanding system of accountability" (descriptive belief). It should be fairly easy to see that these latter variables are all relevant and need to be identified for you to adequately deal with resistance.

In the above example, the descriptive belief about self is probably the core cause of the resistance. Therefore, if you only dealt with the stated evaluative belief and never identified the more basic descriptive belief, it is unlikely that the resistance would dissipate. In contrast to many real-life situations, this example is fairly uncomplicated. In actual practice, I recommend that you not belabor efforts to identify a "core" cause. Frequently, it will be difficult and maybe even impossible to do so because key variables in a cluster never surface. Also, in most cases, you are dealing with small groups of employees, not with individuals, and each of them could have a unique cluster. Try your best to uncover as many variables as possible. Through this process, you will usually be able to identify enough causes to have a significant impact on the resistance.

You should also be aware that there are different reasons people say something in trying to resist change. Sometimes people deliberately mention a fact, belief, or value to disguise the real reason for their resistance. Going back to the example given above, the evaluative belief about management by objectives may be presented in a calculated move to keep the descriptive belief about oneself hidden.

At other times, people may sincerely hold a fact, belief, or value stated to resist change and be unaware of the connection between this and other unstated facts, beliefs, and values. In either case, it is a good idea to gather as much information as possible about these unstated variables because it may be necessary to deal with them before the resistance can be lowered. The most effective way to gather the additional information you need is to ask nonthreatening questions relevant to the specific situation. The questions should convey to your employees that you are genuinely interested in helping them. Some examples are:

- Can you tell me any other reasons why you don't think we should make this change?

- Do you see anything positive that could happen if we change this?

- Can you think of ways that we could make this change easier on employees?

- Do you see any alternatives to this change that might be better?

- How can I help you implement this change?

- Tell me what you like best about your job.

So far I've been talking about resistance indicated by something a person says. Sometimes, however, employees will listen attentively as you announce a change without expressing any opposition, but fail to implement it. This silent resistance is frequently an effective way to get you to abandon the change. Obviously, your primary clue that the change is being resisted is that nothing happens. There are times when this form of resistance represents a conspiracy among employees ("Don't pay any attention to him. He'll forget about it in a few days"), while at other times it may be due, for instance, to a lack of adequate instructions. To determine why the change has not been implemented, however, you need to follow up by asking employees about the progress they are making, or about any difficulties they are having implementing the change. This verbal interaction should help you identify whether or not the problem stems from resistance.

Having done your best to identify causes of resistance, it is now time to decide what to do about them. Part IV will provide guidelines for reducing resistance and preparing the path of least resistance.

PART IV

Dealing with Resistance

Characteristics of Effective **10** *Change Strategies*

There are several general factors characteristic of most effective change strategies. They may sound simplistic or even corny — you may form that evaluative belief. Nonetheless, most of them are present in real organizations where change occurs naturally and with powerful results.

Develop a Positive Climate for Change

The beliefs that your employees have about you and the work environment under normal circumstances will affect their responses during times of change. Your employees will begin developing a set of beliefs about you and the work environment from the very moment they are employed. If these beliefs are basically positive, they will tend to aid efforts during change. If, however, the beliefs are negative, they could be instrumental in establishing a "climate of resistance" which tends to interfere with any efforts to initiate change. If you want employees to support you during times of change, you need to establish the groundwork for this by demonstrating to them, under routine working conditions, that you are a fair and reasonable person who has their best interests in mind.

Encourage an Interest in Improvement

The chances of successfully initiating change will be greater if you have established conditions under which your employees want to do their best. If employees don't care about achievement or their own development, there will be less incentive for them to change. A "why bother" attitude may surface, which militates against any change. On the other hand, if you have helped them cultivate an interest in systematically improving their abilities and performance — a process which in itself requires change — they will tend to be more supportive of other types of changes you initiate. Thus, the general level of readiness to change among employees will tend to be greater if previous changes have been personally rewarding and, therefore, positively reinforced.

Show Your Employees How Change Can Help Them

Readiness to change will tend to be greater if you can convince employees that the change will leave them better off than they are right now. Sometimes this is impossible. You may have to implement a decision made higher in the organization which will have a negative effect on some or all employees. When that is the case, be honest about it. Otherwise you won't be believed on other occasions.

It is psychologically safer for people to stay the way they are than to risk the uncertainty brought about by something new. Frequently, people would rather stay with the known than venture into the unknown, even if the known keeps them from developing their potential. When change is proposed, people see the possibility for improvement, but they also see the possibility that their situation could become worse. It is normal and adaptive for people to weigh the pros and cons of any change before making it. Therefore, if you want to prepare the way for change, you should try to lower uncertainty by showing employees how the change can benefit them.

Help Employees Increase Their Competence

Change will tend to be more successful if it provides employees with opportunities to increase their competence through real accomplishments. In chapter 2, I said that a belief in one's competence must be based on actual achievements in order to be "real." Any change can increase or decrease the beliefs people have regarding their competence. Since competence is a need that most people try to fulfill, they will be more supportive of a change if they view it as an opportunity to become more competent. In addition, people who firmly believe in their competence will probably be more receptive to change than people who question their competence.

Involve Your Employees in Change Decisions

Generally, people have a more difficult time adjusting to change initiated by others because they have less control over the processes involved, and it is more difficult for them to anticipate how the change might affect them. Because of these factors, change initiated by others generally creates more uncertainty for people than change which they initiate themselves. Whenever you begin to initiate change, remember that people's first consideration will be focused on how the change will affect them personally. Whether they support you or resist you will depend greatly on the beliefs they establish as they try to anticipate the impact of the change on their lives.

Also, it is a basic psychological principle that people will be more supportive of changes they are involved in making. The issue here is one of determining who the change belongs to. If you make the decision without involving those who will be affected by it, the change belongs to you. Therefore, if the change isn't successful, the failure also belongs to you. If you involve those who will be affected in decision making, the change belongs to everyone. Employees will more readily commit themselves to changes which belong to them, and since they have a stake in the results, they will be more motivated to insure that the change is a success.

Relate the Change to Your Employee's Values

People will be more apt to support a change if it increases the time they have to pursue their values. Therefore, if the change will provide more opportunities for people to pursue values they regard as important, it is less likely that resistance will be encountered.

Develop a Value for Teamwork

There is a higher probability that employees will work in harmony to implement change if the work environment is structured so that they need each other to carry out their various job functions. When people need each other to accomplish work assignments, it is easier for them to develop values for cooperation, teamwork, negotiation, compromise, and so on. Values such as these will be helpful to you in bringing about any kind of change which requires employees to work together toward a common goal. This, of course, includes almost any kind of change you can think of. Therefore, demonstrate, through what you say and do, that you place a high premium on the willingness of your employees to cooperate.

Avoid Direct Confrontations with Employees

It is usually more effective to subtly work to prepare people for change, than it is to openly confront them with the ways in which their facts, beliefs, and values are causing resistance. Remember that people want to believe that their facts, beliefs, and values are valid. Therefore, a direct challenge could create defensiveness. For example, it would be risky to confront someone by saying, "You don't want to do this because you have a negative self-concept."

When people become defensive, their readiness to change fades as they struggle to protect the integrity of their personality. The irony here is that the more accurate your analysis, the more likely an open confrontation will lead to defensiveness. The reason for this is that a serious threat to established facts, beliefs, or values backs a person into a corner, and they may become very irrational and emotional in their efforts to get out ("Well, if that's what you think of me, I quit!").

Although a direct confrontation can sometimes be very effective ("Gee, I never realized I was doing that"), I regard it as a high-risk strategy which can easily bring negative results. It is not uncommon for a confrontation to make a situation worse than it was originally, and greatly impede the process of lowering resistance. For these reasons, I recommend that you try to avoid this type of strategy.

Debates Are Risky

It is often unproductive to develop a strategy based on debating the validity of specific facts, beliefs, and values with your employees. People can always supply evidence to substantiate their facts, beliefs, and values. Although you may see loopholes in their logic, a debate is a high-risk strategy that can put people on the defensive. You can tell if people are ready to benefit from a debate if they objectively listen to what you have to say. As soon as they start arguing, however, this method ceases to be productive, and you should abandon it for another approach.

Another problem with a debate over the validity of facts, beliefs, and values is that there is a good chance you will lose. People have had years to polish and refine their facts, beliefs, and values, and they will be able to counter just about anything you throw at them. If you persist in a debate to prove a point, you may end up winning the battle, but losing the war against resistance. People may come away from such a debate with a stronger commitment to their facts, beliefs, and values than they had to begin with, even though it is precisely these personality components which are responsible for the resistance. Approaches which do not *directly* call attention to specific facts, beliefs, and values tend to be more effective. Of course, there are exceptions to this, and in any specific situation you will have to exercise considerable judgment in determining whether or not employees are ready to benefit from a debate. (I will have more to say about how you make such judgments in the next chapter.)

Don't React Emotionally

One of the common mistakes made by managers when they encounter resistance is to become angry, frustrated, impatient, or exasperated. This type of emotional response is understandable since managers, like everyone else, are only human. The problem with an emotional reaction, however, is that it increases the probability that the resistance will intensify. In fact, you may actually give people more reasons to show resistance than they had originally.

Remember that anger directed toward others is likely to make them afraid or angry in return, which tends to decrease their readiness to change. This could create a pattern in which initial resistance is encountered, followed by hostility and, inevitably, more resistance. Needless to say, this is a self-defeating cycle which you should try to avoid.

In dealing with resistance, it is much more effective to be objective and descriptive than judgmental and critical. Put your emotions to one side, and try to look at resistance logically by systematically attempting to understand what others are saying and doing. This will help you keep the focus of your attention on the factors causing resistance, rather than on your reaction to it.

Avoid Inadvertent Mistakes

Sometimes managers can be their own worst enemy by doing or saying something that inadvertently intensifies resistance. Some examples of things to avoid doing are: offering advice or making a decision before gaining a full understanding of all relevant factors; making a change based on your understanding of a problem, without checking to see if others concur with your assessment; criticizing an employee in front of others; and showing insensitivity to the feelings of your employees. Some examples of statements you should avoid making are:

- In spite of what you think, the real problem is . . .

- Your analysis of the situation is totally wrong. The factors you should be considering are . . .

- I had a problem like that once myself, and what you should do is . . .

- This situation may seem difficult to you, but actually it's quite simple.

- This is a very touchy issue. You better let me handle it.

Concentrate on Factors within Your Control

In developing a strategy, concentrate your attention on factors over which you can exercise some control. It is a waste of time for you to become frustrated because there are aspects of a situation you can't do anything about. Many managers use such factors as organizational policies and procedures to excuse themselves from doing something about resistance. If you carefully study a situation, however, there are almost always some things you can do to lower resistance. For best results, identify these factors and invest your time and energy in dealing with them.

The
Resistance
Strategy **11**
Model

The resistance strategy model (see figure 3) is intended to take you step by step through a situation in which resistance to change is either anticipated or has already surfaced. As I describe in detail the six steps in the resistance strategy model, I plan to illustrate points made in previous chapters to clarify and firmly tie together all issues relevant to dealing with resistance. After reviewing these six steps, you should *believe* that your knowledge and skills are more fully developed and *want* to use this approach the next time a change is contemplated. I hope to convince you of the practical utility of the model, and thereby lower any *resistance* you may have to using it.

Uses and Limitations

Change is inevitable; nothing remains the same whether or not we are aware of it. The question is the role that we play in controlling the process by which change is brought about. Obviously, you will have little or no control over change if you don't know anything about it. If your superiors are contemplating a change and you are left out of decision making, your control over the process will be limited. There will also be times when you are involved in discussions regarding change, but disagree with the final decision of what the change will consist of and how it will be implemented. We are all put in situations where we must carry out changes we don't agree with. Economic considerations, technological advances, the demand for services or supplies, and other factors may force an organization to make changes which affect all employees. It may be little consolation that you are involved in discussions regarding these changes. Implementing the inevitable weakens the belief that people have some control over their destiny. Sometimes the most we can do is grin and bear the change, hoping that we survive it intact.

The resistance strategy model was not designed to deal with change over which you have no control, although information on developing and implementing strategies may be useful in lowering resistance. Rather, the model has been specifically designed for situations in which you are actively involved in deciding the nature of the change, how it will take place, and the time frame for implementing it. In addition, although the model could be used to deal with resistance deriving from major organizational changes, my concern will focus on day-to-day actions of managers working with superiors and with employees.

Remember, change is necessary for any kind of growth and development to occur, for both individuals and organizations. Since change by its very nature entails modifications in how things are currently handled, there is always adjustment as people get used to these modifications. This is true regardless of the magnitude of the change. Both large and small changes require adjustment, because people will have to alter their view of reality to some extent. And it's

STEP 1:
Define the Change

STEP 2:
Determine the Intensity, Source,
and Focus of Possible Resistance

STEP 3:
Develop the Strategy

STEP 4:
Implement the Strategy

STEP 5:
Evaluate the Results
of the Strategy

STEP 6:
Repeat Steps
2, 3, 4, and 5
as Required

Fig. 3   The Resistance Strategy Model

always a matter of perspective what qualifies as a large or a small change; what seems small to you might be a major trauma to someone else, and vice versa.

The adjustment involved in major changes is frequently more smooth than with small changes. Two people, for example, may show little resistance when asked to change buildings, but tremendous resistance when asked to exchange desks. "It's the small things that'll kill you," suggests the apparent absurdity of situations like this. The mistake here is defining "small" from your own point of view. A good rule of thumb is to look at the meaning of a change from the standpoint of someone who must go through it. The point here is that it is a good idea to use the model even when you believe the desired change to be trivial. This will enable you to avoid problems when a change you believe small turns out to be large. And if it really is small, the use of it won't take much time.

Before you can do anything, you need to determine what it is you want to change. There are a variety of decision-making models which can be used to determine that a change is necessary; however, discussion of these models is beyond the scope of this book. It is also not my purpose to describe how you can evaluate the merits of any proposed change. My major bias along these lines is that whenever possible change should promote the development of human potential. My goal here is to outline an approach for dealing with resistance which can be used once you have decided what you want to change.

Step One: Define the Change

It is important for you to be as concrete, complete, and precise as possible in delineating what you want to change. Often, managers state the desired change in vague or general terms; they describe a direction rather than an end. If things do not turn out as they intended, they feel frustrated and think they are encountering resistance when confusion is the only obstacle to change. Know the concrete outcome you want and state it clearly.

Another common mistake is to define the change only in terms of the *end* result. Most changes involve more than one step. They occur within systems in which the final desired change requires a series of small changes. It is easy for managers, in the press of events, to look only at the desired end. If you want to minimize resistance, you must define the intended change as completely as possible. Otherwise, when faced with resistance, you may wrongly conclude that your goal is being resisted when in fact one small step is the source of the problem. And there may be some easy alternatives to that step.

Even when they have defined the change as concretely and completely as possible, managers occasionally fail to specify the sequence and timing of the change. This can result in a frustrating tangle of effort and the frustration may foster or strengthen resistance.

Step Two: Determine Intensity, Source, and Focus of Possible Resistance

After you define the intended change, determine who will be affected by the change and anticipate how they will respond to it. Ideally, you will be able to predict resistance in advance and take steps to prevent it. Since any change involves adjustment, however, some resistance can usually be expected. Of course, the intensity of resistance can extend from little to extreme. If resistance can't be prevented entirely, the next most desirable outcome is for you to keep it minimal.

Recall that resistance is a three-dimensional phenomenon which will take different forms depending upon its intensity, source, and focus. The intensity of resistance can vary tremendously, and the source can combine facts, descriptive beliefs, evaluative beliefs, or values which focus on oneself, others, or the situation. Part III was devoted to showing how to identify resistance from what people say and do. The most important points to remember are: any fact, belief, or value will either tend to promote or interfere with someone's readiness to change; and accurate identification of the intensity, source, and focus of actual or potential resistance is necessary before a strategy can be developed to deal with it. Like putting together puzzle pieces, the more evidence you can gather from what people say and do, the better you will be able to separate causes from symptoms and correctly identify the reasons for resistance.

As you do this, keep in mind that there is never too much evidence. Since you must infer facts, beliefs, and values from what people say and do, collect as much evidence as possible before drawing any inferences. The inventory, described earlier, can save you much time. In addition, always regard your inferences as hypotheses open to modification based on additional evidence. You cannot afford to develop a vested interest in any of your inferences. An incorrect inference may be worse than none. Besides, your goal is to lower resistance, not to prove that you are right. You can avoid some needless mistakes if you keep this uppermost in your mind.

Step Three: Develop the Strategy

After you have clearly identified the intensity, source, and focus of actual or potential resistance, the next step is to develop a strategy or plan designed to deal with that type of resistance. A philosophical and moral question becomes relevant at this point: What right do you have to tamper with the beliefs and values of other people? This is an extremely important question—one that often immobilizes managers. My answer is that we have every right to tamper with beliefs and values; the issue is not whether we should do this, but how we do it.

Everything you do or say to employees *right now* has an impact on their values and beliefs. There is no such thing as a neutral action. Your effect may be large or small, intended or unintended, but your employees will be altered in some way every time you have contact with them. Since a change in values and beliefs will leave them better or worse off than before, you have a responsibility to insure that you are as constructive as possible.

There is no magic formula for dealing with resistance. Even if your strategy is extremely well thought out, something can always go wrong. Every situation is unique, and human behavior is simply too complex to predict the outcome of any strategy with certainty. In developing strategies, we are limited to thinking of them in terms of the probability that they will be successful. For any given instance of resistance, there will always be a number of viable options. Your job is to thoroughly evaluate the pros and cons of each alternative and select the one with the highest probability of success, given all available evidence. To aid in doing this, you can tailor a strategy to a specific instance of resistance.

The first step in this process is to generate specific ideas from the gathered evidence, and second, you need to formulate as many alternative strategies as possible based on all your specific ideas. Let's take a closer look at these two important steps.

Generate Specific Ideas from the Evidence

I have indicated that you can infer the facts, descriptive beliefs, evaluative beliefs, and values of people by listening to what they say and observing what they do. Each individual can express or show resistance through one or a combination of these four basic sources. If more than one employee is involved, resistance may come from a complex variety of sources at the same time. When this is the case, you need to develop your strategy so that you can deal with several different kinds of resistance simultaneously.

Now let me indicate some questions you can ask yourself when generating ideas from the evidence you have gathered regarding facts, descriptive beliefs, evaluative beliefs, and values:

FACTS

- Does the statement meet the definition of a fact — is it based on empirical evidence?

- If so, have all facts relevant to the situation been identified?

- If the statement is not a fact, is it a descriptive belief (an interpretation regarding what is correct or incorrect), an evaluative belief (an interpretation regarding what is good or bad), or a value (a belief regarding what is worth pursuing in life)?

- Does the fact promote or interfere with the person's ability or willingness to develop potential to the fullest extent possible?

- If the results of people's facts are negative, if they are paralyzed by the past, how can they be helped to look at present and future opportunities positively?

DESCRIPTIVE BELIEFS

- Is the descriptive belief based on accurate or inaccurate facts or interpretations?

- If the descriptive belief is based on inaccurate facts or interpretations, how can it be corrected?

- Does the descriptive belief promote or interfere with the person's ability or willingness to develop potential to the fullest extent possible?

- If the results of descriptive beliefs are negative, how can this be changed?

EVALUATIVE BELIEF

- What facts or descriptive beliefs form the foundation for the evaluative belief in question?

- Are those facts or descriptive beliefs accurate or inaccurate?

- If they are inaccurate, how can they be corrected?

- Does the evaluative belief promote or interfere with the person's ability or willingness to develop potential to the fullest extent possible?

- If the results of using evaluative beliefs are negative, how can this be changed?

VALUE

- Is the value based on any stated facts or descriptive beliefs?

- If so, are the facts or descriptive beliefs accurate or inaccurate?

- If they are inaccurate, how can they be corrected?

- Is the value based on any evaluative beliefs?

- Are the effects of these evaluative beliefs positive or negative?

- If they are negative, how can this be changed?

- Does the value promote or interfere with the person's ability or willingness to develop potential to the fullest extent possible?

● If the results of pursuing the value are negative, how can this be changed?

As you answer these questions, the type of resistance in a situation will become clearer, and you can start to see what factors need to be considered in developing a strategy. Note that few of the listed questions can be objectively verified. Most of the questions require subjective inferences. This is why I have stressed gathering as much evidence as possible. Due to the intangible nature of the variables, you may have to rely completely on subjective inferences. Nevertheless, this method can be very useful, if you do everything possible to check and double check your data.

Formulate Alternative Strategies

(Note: You may want to read some or all of the case studies in chapter 12 along with this section.) After identifying specific ideas based on your data regarding facts, descriptive beliefs, evaluative beliefs, and values, the next step is to take all this information and formulate as many potential strategies as you can think of. Try to be as creative as possible in developing alternative strategies, so that you don't prematurely rule out an approach which might be effective. You will have time later to assess each potential strategy in terms of its probability of reducing resistance.

In developing potential strategies, keep in mind that a strong relationship exists between a person's facts, descriptive beliefs, evaluative beliefs, and values, on the one hand, and behavior, on the other. Accordingly, change in one of these variables will lead to changes in the other variables. So, *your strategy should start where people are most receptive to change and build from there.* Discovering where a person's receptiveness to change is greatest will require experimentation on your part. Remember that change in one variable only remotely related to the cause of resistance can lead to changes which have an impact on variables highly significant in causing the resistance. Changes in behavior, for example, can change beliefs about one's competencies, which can then change values about what one wants to do, and vice versa.

Also remember that at any given time a person will be more receptive to change in one variable compared to others. A common mistake by managers is developing a strategy around a variable which is not receptive to change. It is a waste of time, for example, to try to change someone's value, if the person staunchly defends that value. If the value causes resistance to something you want to do, but is not amenable to change, then your strategy should focus on modifying a fact, descriptive belief, evaluative belief, or behavior, which can then have an impact on the value in question.

The next most frequent mistake in dealing with resistance is to fail to modify a strategy as receptiveness to change shifts from one variable to another. The interplay between facts, beliefs, values and behavior is very dynamic and fluid. People are constantly exposed to new experiences that have an impact on their entire personality. One day a person may be very receptive to change in a belief, but the next day resist such change. Therefore, your strategy will only be effective to the extent that it is flexible. By listening to what people say and observing what they do, you can see how receptiveness to change shifts among facts, values, beliefs, and behavior. As this occurs, the probability of successfully dealing with resistance depends upon your ability to shift your strategy.

To demonstrate how you can formulate alternative strategies to deal with resistance, let's say that you want to transfer one of your employees to another department where his skills are in greater need, but you know he believes he would have problems adjusting to another group of coworkers. Therefore, his resistance stems from a descriptive belief he holds about himself. You need to brainstorm several alternative strategies that might lower his resistance. Some possible strategies are:

- Simply tell him that he is going to be transferred.

- Give him the choice of going to the other department or staying where he is with little chance for promotion.

- Talk to him about his belief to see if there is any way you can help him change it.

- Tell him he has the choice of either being transferred or leaving the company.

- Tell him you have decided to transfer him, but will let him work part-time here and part-time in the other department for six months, so that he can gradually adjust to the change.

- Let him know he is needed in the other department and that you expect him to do his best to adjust to the change.

- Tell him that his belief is ridiculous and that he should get rid of it.

- Suggest that he try the new assignment on a temporary ninety-day basis.

Once you have generated as many potential strategies as possible, you need to weigh the pros and cons of each alternative, then select the one that has the highest probability of lowering resistance. In this example, you may conclude that given all relevant factors, the best option is to tell this employee that you have decided to transfer him for a ninety-day trial period. You may select this option because you *believe* it has the advantage of reducing fear while avoiding certain disadvantages which might result from the other options. Notice the emphasis given to the word *believe*. A strategy is nothing more than your best guess regarding how to deal with resistance. Although you can use the methods suggested in this book to increase the probability of success, there is never a guarantee that your strategy will be effective. There are risks associated with any strategy — everything you say or do will raise or lower the level of resistance.

Facing this kind of uncertainty, doing nothing may seem an attractive option, and this is a potential strategy which should be considered along with others. Before using this method, however, determine whether it is the best available, given the specific situation you are faced with. Unfortunately, some managers elect to do nothing because they don't know what to do or they're afraid to act. I'm sure you've heard people say, "Wait a few days and the problem will take care of itself." It is unlikely that serious resistance will simply disappear through time. Doing nothing frequently gives it time to intensify. The cold, hard reality is that most cases of resistance will require active intervention on your part.

Step Four: Implement the Strategy

In implementing a strategy, the two most important factors to consider are timing and pacing. Timing has to do with when you implement the strategy. An adequate strategy may intensify resistance simply because it was introduced at the wrong time. Of course, it is no easy task to determine when the best time is; and to complicate matters, it is possible to be either too early or too late. The receptiveness of people to your strategy will be greater at some times than at others, depending upon what else is going on in their lives.

The best way to increase the accuracy of your timing is to know all employees as well as possible and be familiar with how they respond under varied circumstances. If you know, for example, that your employees just found out they aren't going to receive an expected pay raise, now might not be a good time to deal with their resistance concerning changes in work assignments. There will probably be greater receptiveness to this if you wait until tomorrow or next week. In a similar manner, personal, interpersonal, or situational variables either related or unrelated to a proposed change need to be considered in deciding when to implement a strategy. This will increase the probability that your strategy will be successful.

Pacing, which is related to timing, has to do with how much of your strategy to introduce at any given time. Even people receptive to change have limits to how much they can handle within a given time span, since any change involves adjustment. If you push people, you could inadvertently create resistance which wasn't there. This could compound troubles if you are trying to implement a strategy to deal with resistance already present. Just don't defeat yourself by going too fast. If employees begin to show signs of anxiety or resentment, this is a clue that you should look at the pace of implementing the strategy. Since individuals will vary in their responses to your strategy, you will need to go slower with some people than with others. If you allow for these individual differences and modify the pace accordingly, the effectiveness of your strategy will be greatly enhanced.

Step Five: Evaluating the Results of the Strategy

Evaluating the effectiveness of your strategy is important in successfully dealing with resistance. Remember that evaluation is not a one-step procedure which is completed after the strategy has been implemented. Rather, it is an ongoing process which begins from the moment you start implementing your strategy and continues until the resistance is reduced as much as possible. All through the implementation phase, what people say and do will tell you whether or not your strategy is working. Sometimes your attempts to deal with resistance will lead to dramatic results which are clearly positive or negative. Often, however, the results will show up in small changes difficult to recognize. In their zeal to lower resistance, some managers overlook or play down small changes. They may even abandon a good strategy if it doesn't meet with immediate and dramatic success.

You can avoid this mistake by keeping in mind that even small changes in a value, belief, or behavior can be a significant sign that your strategy is working. Since these elements are interrelated, even a small change may be the beginning of a process which eventually yields significant results. Therefore, notice any positive changes, regardless of magnitude, and nurture them to the fullest.

Step Six: Repeat Steps Two through Five, as Required

Since any strategy is a hypothesis about how to lower resistance, you will not know if it is working until you begin to implement it. Therefore, the results of your ongoing evaluation will be your major resource if you need to modify your approach. Rarely will you be able to develop and implement a strategy without making adjustments. Be prepared to make mistakes and to deal with them as needed. Some frequent mistakes are:

- Incorrectly assessing the intensity, source, and focus of resistance

- Basing your strategy on a symptom rather than the cause of resistance

- Failing to consider all relevant factors in developing the strategy

- Implementing a strategy not well suited to the situation

- Failing to adjust the strategy to account for new information

- Implementing the strategy at the wrong time or at an unrealistic pace

In addition, your strategy may have consequences you could not have anticipated. Your strategy may backfire, causing more problems than you had originally. The cause of resistance may change when you are in the middle of implementing your strategy, or employees may confront you with counterstrategies which complicate the entire process. For all these reasons, any time you are faced with a setback or failure, you need to repeat steps two through five as often as necessary to accomplish your objectives. The biggest error you can make is to assume your strategy is correct and stick with it, in spite of evidence to the contrary. The only way you can beat resistance is to be flexible enough to *change* your own strategy when it appears that another approach would be more effective.

Application of the 12 *Resistance Strategy Model*

Case Studies

In this chapter, I will present ten brief case studies showing how the resistance strategy model can be used to deal with resistance in varied situations. Although there is no way to present all potential uses of the model, since every situation is unique, sample case studies may help you see how you might use the model. Although I have found this model most useful in dealing with resistance in individuals and small groups, it could also be used with larger groups. However, keeping track of all relevant facts, beliefs, values, and behavior would be more complicated. Therefore, I will confine examples to less complex situations where the model's practical utility is greater and easier to understand.

The Misunderstanding

Nat Reed was manager of an engineering department that develops modular electronic components. In this particular company, engineers working in teams of two had proven to be most productive. Of ten teams, all but one, Bill Riley and Mike Crane, were on schedule for project deadlines. Since Bill and Mike frequently argued, they were behind schedule and jeopardized a large project's success. When Nat talked with them jointly, they began a shouting match, blaming each other for delays. Not sure how he should handle this, the manager simply told them to speed it up or he would be forced to consider more serious action.

Despite this, Bill and Mike's problem grew worse. Nat considered reassigning them to other teams, but all the other engineers worked well together. Since a heavy production schedule would not allow time to train new engineers, he was reluctant to fire them. Therefore, the only viable alternative was to get at the root of the problem and attempt to resolve it.

Nat searched for clues to how the conflict began. He talked to other engineers in the department and to Bill and Mike separately. Through this process, he found that the problem began before the two were assigned to work together. Someone told Bill that Mike drove off his last partner because he preferred working alone. Bill feared that Mike would also try to get rid of him (descriptive belief) and was defensive around Mike from the beginning. Someone also told Mike that Bill was assigned to work with him even though he preferred to work with someone else. So he believed that Bill did not want to work with him (descriptive belief), which made him defensive also.

The resistance which prevented the two engineers from accepting their team assignment stemmed from descriptive beliefs they had about each other that were never checked for accuracy. Nat learned when talking with Mike that his last partner left because he was unhappy about his salary and opportunities for advancement. He also found that Mike preferred working with a partner. In a separate talk with Bill, Nat discovered that he preferred working with a close friend, but did not object to working with Mike until he was told that Mike drove off his last partner. Nat brought the two together to help clarify misunderstandings. Both were surprised and relieved to find that initial beliefs about each other were unfounded. After this clarification, they began to work harmoniously and their production increased.

The New System
for Monitoring Expenditures

Marie Shepard, manager of purchasing and supply, annually submitted budget estimates for the next year's supplies. Because she underestimated expenditures for the last two months of a previous budget, she exceeded the budget by 10%. Extra funds were taken from another department's budget, and people in accounting took time from other responsibilities to straighten this out. Because of this problem, Marie's supervisor asked her to devise a better way of keeping track of expenditures, so that she would not run short again.

Marie reviewed systems for monitoring expenditures and selected the one which proved most successful in companies similar to hers. She developed procedures to implement the new system and introduced it at a weekly staff meeting. Although Marie was excited about the system, the staff didn't share her enthusiasm. They expressed considerable resistance toward the procedures. Most considered the current system the best available (evaluative belief) and felt that there was no need to change it. Several argued that the budget problem of the previous year wouldn't occur again (descriptive belief).

Based on the reports she read, Marie was convinced that the new system had definite advantages over current procedures. Before it could be successfully implemented, she needed to overcome her staff's resistance. In thinking through their reluctance, she could not find any reason for resistance except their preferring the status quo. Therefore, she needed to encourage them to want the new system rather than the old. She recalled that two people showed less resistance than others during the staff meeting, but went along with the group. So she asked them to implement the system as a pilot test to see if it was more effective than the old. They agreed.

After six months, both employees were enthusiastic about the new system. It helped them keep better track of expenditures, while cutting down on paperwork. Other employees gradually became interested in using the new system; their evaluative belief about the old system changed. Marie concluded that she might have been more successful at first if she had involved the staff in selecting a new system. Since she chose it, assuming that its merits would be obvious, their resistance caught her off guard. She needed to reassess matters to encourage them to adopt the system. The pilot test saved her from being forced to order implementation of the new system, over staff objections.

The Supervisory Training Controversy

Ed Stewart was director of staff development. Plans for new training programs were approved by a staff development committee, consisting of three company vice presidents. A recent study showed that 90% of the new supervisors were promoted from the ranks, and it took about two years before their production reached that of experienced supervisors. New supervisors received informal on-the-job training, but Ed felt they could increase production sooner if the company had a structured supervisory training program.

When Ed presented this idea to the staff development committee, one vice president strongly opposed him, saying, "We're obviously not selecting qualified people. A training program would be a waste of money" (descriptive belief).

The other two vice presidents were open to the idea, and postponed a decision until the next meeting. They asked Ed to provide them with additional justification at that time.

After thinking about the meeting and the vice president's opposition, Ed began considering options. He concluded that it would be difficult to obtain sufficient data to counter the belief that the selection procedure was the main problem. He decided instead to attempt to demonstrate that a training program could provide additional benefits. He knew that the vice president opposing him was reasonable and could be persuaded by logical evidence.

Ed reviewed professional literature dealing with the effects of supervisory training programs on production, as well as turnover rates, grievances, and absenteeism. He also gathered information from companies with similar programs. After summarizing collected data (facts), Ed made a convincing presentation at the next staff development committee meeting. These facts supplemented the "fact" given by the one member, so the committee unanimously authorized the program.

Performance Evaluation Procedures Under Attack

Pete Moreno, manager of data processing, had six first-line supervisors reporting directly to him. During the past five years, complaints filed against these supervisors increased. Not sure why this happened, Pete met with representative employees in the department asking for suggestions. They recommended more employee involvement in routine performance evaluations of supervisors. Thinking that this was a good idea, he and the company's industrial psychologist developed an instrument for rating supervisors on job-related dimensions.

Although this procedure could be useful in identifying correctable deficiencies and reducing grievances, the six supervisors resisted it. They said that it would undermine their authority and give unhappy employees opportunity to vent hostility at supervisors (descriptive beliefs). Pete explained that the instrument would be a learning tool, and that he could recognize unfounded criticism. The supervisors still opposed the idea. Pete promised to consider the matter further and discuss it with them again at a future meeting.

Pete suggested that the reasons stated for opposition were not the only ones. He felt fairly certain that the supervisors feared that critical comments by employees on the instrument might put their jobs in jeopardy, that the evaluation results would harm them rather than help them.

After considering alternatives, he focused his strategy on one supervisor on probation because of employee complaints. Pete gave the supervisor the choice of trying the new evaluation or being demoted. This supervisor agreed, convinced that demotion was imminent anyway (descriptive belief). When the evaluation came back, Pete and the supervisor discovered deficiencies the supervisor was unaware of. From this information, they jointly planned ways to correct these deficiencies. Within three months, the supervisor improved and was removed from probation. This particular supervisor, previously against the method, now spoke highly of it. Other supervisors agreed to try it. After experience with the method, anxiety about job security evaporated, and evaluations became routine. Grievances were reduced, and the relationship between supervisors and employees improved.

The Employee Who Feared Promotion

Barbara Hunter, an effective interviewer in the personnel department for three years, had a master's in business administration. In talks with her supervisor, Judy Hall, she indicated strong interest in management. Judy told her that she had the necessary educational background, but would need management training to adequately prepare for advancement. The organization offered an intensive training program for those aspiring to management, and since Barbara met criteria for this program, Judy suggested she take it. Judy told her that she would recommend her for the program and provide whatever assistance she needed. Barbara enthusiastically enrolled.

The first training sessions gave an overview of approaches to management, and Barbara felt comfortable. When training shifted to simulated problem solving requiring active participation, Barbara had difficulty. Because she felt inadequate in her ability to succeed as a manager (evaluative belief), she finished the course but showed no interest in applying for available management positions. When Judy asked about this, she said that she preferred personnel work to management (bogus value).

Remembering how enthusiastic Barbara was about management, Judy was puzzled by the sudden change. When asked about this, Barbara explained her problems in the course and said she felt inadequate to take on management responsibilities While her manager argued that she shouldn't form a conclusion based solely on the experience in the course, Barbara was not persuaded. She concluded that she would fail as a manager and closed it off as a career possibility.

After this discussion, Judy formed a strategy to deal with Barbara's resistance. She knew that initially Barbara was very confident about her potential, although she had no experience to base this on. That's why Judy suggested the management training program. Judy hypothesized that Barbara's untested confidence was shattered during the course, and she jumped to the conclusion that she could never succeed as a manager (inductive fallacy).

Judy decided to gradually provide Barbara experiences ·that might alter her evaluative belief about her management potential. She appointed Barbara to represent her on major committees and delegated office managerial duties to her. Barbara began developing management skills which changed her belief about her potential. Within a year, she grew as enthusiastic about management as before, and her confidence was backed by solid experience. She was offered a management position in another division, and became one of the most capable managers in the organization. Although Judy regretted losing Barbara, she was pleased to help someone develop her capabilities.

The Vindictive Employee

Charles Kelly was a skilled machine operator in a metal products company. His manager was John Luboff. One day, John mentioned his displeasure about the quality of work Charles accepted from apprentice machine operators he supervised. Charles became defensive, arguing that work standards were unrealistically high for people with little experience. John was surprised by Charles's defensive response but decided to forget the incident.

Several months later Charles and several other machinists applied for an opening as foreman. When someone else got the position, Charles was furious. He believed that John had given him a bad recommendation because of their discussion about work quality (cause-effect fallacy). He became belligerent and bad-mouthed John to other employees. When John heard this, his first impulse was to fire Charles. To John such behavior was inexcusable. Fortunately, John did not act on his anger and tried to find a rational explanation for Charles's behavior.

John decided to discuss it with Charles. Although Charles was reluctant, he revealed his belief about John. John was surprised because he considered the incident minor and had supported Charles for foreman. When John showed Charles a very favorable reference letter, Charles realized that he was wrong and apologized. Both agreed to avoid future situations like this by more open communication.

If You're a Manager, You're Against Me

Kent Smithson was a new assembly line worker whose manager was Hal Kaubmaun. Where Kent had worked, he was an active union member and had bitter arguments with management over wages and working conditions. He had been fired for this conduct. Because of this experience, Kent believed that management was against labor in any company and would do little to meet their needs (descriptive belief). He also believed that labor had to fight for any improvements in working conditions (descriptive belief). Since this had been true in the past, he concluded that it would also be true under Hal's management (deductive fallacy).

Hal noticed that Kent was somewhat hostile toward him from the beginning. This didn't become an issue until Hal established a committee to recommend improvements in labor management relations. Kent opposed the concept of the committee and led a group that tried to convince laborers that this committee was an effort by management to placate employees without really dealing with the issues. Hal felt that Kent misunderstood his motivation and decided to talk with him. Unfortunately, the meeting went badly. Kent was so convinced that he was right that he wouldn't listen to Hal.

Because of this, Hal decided that he needed to form another strategy to deal with growing resistance toward the committee, that Kent instigated. Realizing that Kent couldn't be talked out of his beliefs, the only viable solution would be for the committee to provide concrete, tangible results. Therefore, he ignored Kent's opposing group and worked on accomplishing definite goals through the committee. After a few months, it became increasingly obvious that Hal was dedicated to improving working conditions, drawing upon employees' suggestions. As major reforms were instituted, resistance toward the committee dwindled rapidly. Soon, only Kent opposed the committee, and even he softened. It was difficult for Kent to maintain his beliefs while facing Hal's behavior. Kent, though still skeptical about managers, no longer functioned as a rebel without a cause.

The Unassertive Employee

Mark Andrews, the only black in marketing, was one of five assistant managers in the department headed by Sara Jackson, who was white. After six months on the job, Mark continued to be very quiet and unassertive. He rarely made suggestions during staff meetings and seemed to accept what others thought best. This troubled Sara because the main function of marketing was to create new, imaginative methods for selling company products.

Sara tried to find out why Mark seemed to resist participation. In conversations with Mark and other employees, she postulated that Mark was quiet because he believed the white employees prejudiced. From this hypothesis, Sara developed a strategy she felt would be effective. She separately asked the five assistant managers to encourage Mark to feel that he belonged. During the next few months everyone encouraged Mark, but he remained quiet and unassertive.

Sara was puzzled by Mark's unchanged behavior. In reviewing the problem, she discovered from Mark's personnel file that, although he had considerable management experience, his background in marketing was limited. This additional evidence helped her form a new hypothesis — Mark's behavior stemmed from inexperience in marketing. During a routine evaluation with Mark, she mentioned concern about his reserved group participation and asked if he felt prepared for the job. Mark admitted that he lacked experience, but said he was quiet during meetings because he believed it was important to listen to other's ideas (value).

Sara agreed with him that it was important to listen, but

that he must also contribute ideas of his own. Mark said that he would work on this.

Within a short time, Mark began participating more in meetings and became more outgoing in asking others for help. He also attended several marketing training programs which stimulated his thinking. In time his contributions became more and more insightful. The importance he had placed on listening had blocked his effectiveness in his new job; his emerging value for expressing his own ideas ultimately made him one of the most vital members of the team.

The Personnel Transfer Issue

Les Martin was manager of the advertising department in a company that recently experienced reduced sales. To solve this problem, top management decided that some people should be moved from advertising to sales. This was the only viable option because advertising was the most overstaffed department and the company did not want to hire people unfamiliar with their products. Les said he could transfer three employees to sales without jeopardizing the advertising program. Top management let Les decide which three employees should tranfer to sales.

In a meeting, Les asked for three volunteers from his staff of ten to transfer to sales. He said that they had already decided to eliminate three positions from advertising, and that all ten could do well in sales. He provided a one-step salary increase as an incentive for transfering. After hearing this, the meeting was silent, without volunteers. Les expected resistance because advertising enjoyed higher status than sales. However, he thought the salary increase would motivate three volunteers to transfer.

When no one volunteered, he asked them to meet him separately, prepared to justify why they should not be transferred. After these meetings, Les felt that three employees in particular, Eduardo, Dick, and Carmen, had weak arguments. All three said they wouldn't be good at sales but gave different reasons for their evaluative beliefs. Eduardo said he had no prior experience (fact). Dick revealed that he failed at a sales job in another company (fact). Carmen said her personality wasn't forceful enough (evaluative belief).

Instead of transferring these three over their objections, Les developed a strategy to lower their resistance, based on information from these meetings. Since Eduardo's belief was inaccurate (he had no evidence), Les offered to let him develop skills by working part-time in sales and part-time in advertising, until he felt ready to move.

He learned that Dick did fail in a sales job very different from the one in this company. He helped Dick see that he couldn't compare his experience with the present opportunity because the two were dissimilar. Dick said he would try the new job.

Although Carmen believed she was not extroverted enough to succeed in sales, she admitted knowing little about the sales jobs in the company. Les arranged for Carmen to meet the sales manager and talk with sales personnel. From this, Carmen discovered that the job didn't require a "back slapper" and was relieved because this changed her concept of her ability to do the job. She looked forward to being in sales.

By developing and implementing a strategy tailored to specific causes of resistance in each case, Les succeeded in transfering all three to the sales department. If he had not taken time to do this, their new manager would have inherited three employees who didn't want to be there.

Divide and Conquer

Sandra Thomas started a commercial art company ten years ago. Business had been good, permitting her to expand to twenty-five employees at three locations. However, business began to decline because the city was not growing as rapidly as it had, and competition was keener.

To prevent cutting staff, Sandra needed a way to revitalize her company. She decided to develop a retail graphic product with good sales potential. After surveying the local market, she found a demand for greeting cards, incorporating local humor. In discussing this with her accountant, both concluded that producing greeting cards could aid the company.

There were three key people on Sandra's management team: Jerry Stephenson (Sales), Martha Gould (Art Director), and Carl Holt (Production). At a regular meeting, Sandra presented the greeting card idea. Although Sandra was excited about it, she encountered strong and unexpected resistance from all three managers. Jerry said producing greeting cards would detract from current efforts to increase sales (descriptive belief). Martha admitted that she wasn't interested in greeting cards and suggested that the company explore other ways of boosting sales (value). Finally, Carl said that the project was too complex to be successful (descriptive belief).

Even though Sandra had provided limited information, all three seemed convinced that the project was unworthy or risky. Since she needed everyone's support for the project, she realized that she had to address each person's concerns. Because Martha's objection was general and vague, Sandra began with her. She suggested to Martha that designing greeting cards might stimulate new creativity and imagination in her staff. After this discussion, Martha began to support her against the others' criticism.

Although concerned with different issues, Jerry and Carl's negative comments seemed to reflect fear that producing greeting cards could jeopardize the company. To reduce these fears, Sandra involved the group in a variation of contingency planning called "down-side planning." The group had used this method in the past and found it effective in making decisions. It involved generating a list of things that might go wrong and developing strategies to deal with each possible negative outcome. In this process, Jerry saw that selling greeting cards would not interfere with selling their other services. Carl discovered that although the project was complex, it could be broken down into distinct tasks that were similar to ones they were already doing.

When contingency planning was over, everyone felt more comfortable with Sandra's idea. However, there was lingering resistance about the company's financial vulnerability. Noticing this, Sandra realized that she was the only management team member who understood all the project's financial ramifications. To correct this, she asked the accountant to explain precisely what the project meant in dollars and cents. After this explanation, all traces of resistance left and everyone was eager to produce greeting cards.

Sandra recognized that she was successful because she identified and dealt with specific causes of resistance expressed by each management team member. Her methods helped modify values and beliefs which could have interfered with the project's implementation.

POSTSCRIPT

Alas, sometimes nothing works. It is possible to be thoroughly familiar with all the principles and techniques in this book or any book on change, and still be unable to lower resistance in a specific situation. On occasion, resistance will be caused by factors over which you have no control, and your efforts to reduce it may be futile. There will also be times when, for reasons impossible to identify and explain, you will be unable to deal with resistance, even though all factors are within your control. In these situations, try everything you can think of. If you fail anyway, learn what you can that can be applied in the future and forget about it. Feeling bad about efforts that don't succeed will get you nowhere and even undermine efforts the next time resistance knocks. When reviewing your career at eighty, you want to be able to honestly say without regrets, "I did the best I could."

REFERENCES

Rokeach, M. *Beliefs, attitudes, and values.* San Francisco: Jossey-Bass, 1968.

Rokeach, M. *The nature of human values.* Glencoe, New York: Free Press, 1973.